A Proud History

For Margot Regen,
one of my dearest
neighbors and classmates,
with much love
and many memories,
Betsy Holloway
May 29, 1998

A Proud History

Durham, North Carolina:
The Story of George Watts School

Betsy Holloway

Foreword by Eli N. Evans

Persimmon Press
Orlando 1998

The text of this book is composed in Baskerville.
Composition, printing, and binding
by
E. O. Painter Printing Company
DeLeon Springs, FL

First Edition
Limited to 750 Copies

Illustrations not credited in the text
are from the author's collection.

Library of Congress Catalog Card Number 98-66444
ISBN: 0-9616500-2-8

Persimmon Press, P.O. Box 536531,
Orlando, Florida 32853-6531

This book was produced in conjunction with the Friends of Watts Street School. All profits from the book's sales will be donated to the Friends for the benefit of the school.

Contents

For my mother

Preface and
Acknowledgments

This book owes its existence to John Satterfield, whose energetic interest, effort, and leadership brought into being, in 1995, the Friends of Watts Street School. One of his first actions as President of the new group was to request that I write a history of the school; as a graduate (Class of '48) who has many fond memories of George Watts and its teachers, I was delighted to take on the project. Both John and his wife Carolyn have been infinitely helpful, encouraging, and patient with all my requests for information, and together they have unearthed a number of sources that I had no idea existed.

The occasional confusion as to the school's correct name owes its existence to the fact that the facility opened in 1916 as Watts Street School; that name remained until 1929, when it was officially changed by the City School Board to George Watts School. Understandably, many older graduates of the school still refer to it as Watts Street School, since that was the name when they attended; and in fact even after the name was officially changed, many students, parents, and teachers continued informally to use the older designation. Both names have been used in this book, depending on the era under discussion.

Together with John and Carolyn Satterfield, my thanks go to Louise Adkins, Margaret McCracken Allen, Beverly Barge, Walter Barge, Carol Barnes, Carrie Black, Helen Brockwell, Ruth Cheek, Frances Mason Clement, Helen Coppridge, Marie Crowder, Eli Evans, Cavett French, Dr. John Glasson, Susan Harward, Mary Esther Harward, Belinda Hayes, Don and Betty Hester, John Huckabee, Tommy Hunt, Bill and Ann Kirkland, Laurance and Eva Kirkland, Kay Lloyd, Steve Massengill, Alice Medlin, Dutton Moore, Madge Nicholson, Kathy Peterson, Bob Rankin, Dorothy Rankin, Gayle Rasberry, Rhodney Reade, Sandra Shaw Reaves, Ben and Snow Roberts, Delia Robinson, Ralph Rogers, Carol Seeley Scott, Frances Airheart Terry, Pat Tilley, Nancy Llewellyn Towe, Larry Umstead, Buddy Whitfield, Nancy Williams, Lawrence Williams, Warren

Williams, and the Durham Public Schools. When quoting former George Watts students, I have included the year of their graduation from George Watts School.

Some of my information about George Watts School was acquired during the early 1980s, when I was doing research for my first book. Mrs. Lorraine Pridgen, then about ninety, provided many recollections of her early life and career, as well as of her four decades at this school; some of that information was used in *Heaven For Beginners*, and has also been included in this account.

Accumulating printed materials to support George Watts's history has been an interesting challenge. It's particularly unfortunate that the school's PTA scrapbooks, conscientiously maintained for many years, have disappeared. Left "in perfect order" in 1962, according to an annoyed and mystified Mrs. Pridgen twenty years after her retirement, the scrapbooks could not be located when I researched the school's history during the early 1980s. They reappeared in 1988, when *Coming Together*, an account of George Watts and Walltown Schools, was produced under the supervision of Dr. Michael Courtney, then Principal of George Watts; but they've now vanished again, and an assiduous search during the past two years has failed to locate them. In their absence, I've relied on other sources, including *Coming Together*, for a number of details, especially of PTA activities and involvement.

In addition, both the Jimmy Cannon and the Lily Nelson Jones Cups—the coveted "Outstanding Boy" and "Outstanding Girl" awards that were presented for many years at George Watts graduations—have disappeared; but with the help of various issues of *Watts High Lights* as well as the Durham newspapers, I've recovered nearly all of the recipients' names up until 1958. No one I've interviewed has known when or why these presentations were discontinued.

Watts High Lights, George Watts School's prizewinning newspaper during the 1930s and 1940s, has been of great value in tracing the school's early history; I'm grateful to all those young editors, reporters, and advisors who so carefully and conscientiously recorded the life of their school. Because of the greater availability of sources for the first half of the school's existence than for the second, the emphasis of *A Proud History* falls more heavily on the earlier time than upon the later. Generally speaking, I have indicated information sources within the text rather than in separate notes.

John Satterfield has spent much time and effort in helping me to locate printed materials: in addition to unearthing several bound volumes of early *Watts High Lights*, he discovered the existence of Miss Lily Nelson Jones's personal scrapbook. Thanks to the generosity of "Miss Lily's" niece, Louise Adkins, John provided me with a copy of the entire scrapbook, which proved invaluable in supplying information on the school and the Durham community during the 1920s and 1930s. Frances Airheart Terry was kind enough to supply me with a number of PTA-related materials, as well as contacting several friends in an effort to locate others. Steve Massengill took the time to help me locate materials available through the Division of Archives and History in Raleigh; these have been especially helpful in providing "time capsule" looks at the school from the 1930s through 1970. Ruth Cheek, Helen Coppridge, Mary Esther Harward, and Rhodney Reade contributed copies of *Watts High Lights*, while Kay Lloyd, Ralph Rogers, and Bob Rankin provided me with copies of their commencement programs. Mrs. Harward also lent me her George Watts *Self-Study Report of 1974*, which helped to shed light on a period that is otherwise not well documented. Dr. Ralph Coonrad has given support, help, and encouragement to our entire family while this book was being written, and we are most grateful.

Larry Umstead of the Durham Public Schools has been exceedingly kind in supplying the volumes of Minutes of the City Board of Education, as well as providing space in the Fuller Building for me to study them. It should be noted that City and County school systems remained separate in Durham for 110 years, until they combined in 1992 to form a new entity, the Durham Public Schools.

Helen Coppridge, Eli Evans, Dr. John Glasson, Mary Esther Harward, Carol Seeley Scott, and Warren Williams have been especially thoughtful and generous with their recollections; and I'm grateful to them, as I am to everyone who has helped.

Foreword

by

Eli N. Evans

Durham is so blessed to have a writer like Betsy Holloway, with a passion for the heartbeat of her hometown and the people and institutions that nurtured its children. In this gift of a book, she has painted the portrait of the oldest school structure in the city—built in 1916—with a line of drama and personalities that have animated almost the entire 20th century of the Trinity Park neighborhood. It is the story of a neighborhood that grew up around Trinity College and then Duke University, a community of parents who really cared about their children's education.

It is also the story of scores of teachers—among them the legendary Lily Nelson Jones, who was a teacher and principal for twenty-seven years (principal from 1924 to 1940); Lorraine Pridgen, teacher and principal for forty-five years (principal from 1945 to 1962); Elizabeth Gray, a first grade teacher for forty-one years (from 1919 to 1958); Mary Esther Williams Harward, who taught third grade for thirty-four years (1945-79); and so many others, such as my second grade teacher, Ida Cowan, who lived just down the street from me on Dacian Avenue; Helen Brown, who nurtured me throughout the sixth grade—which she taught from about 1922 until 1958—and many others mentioned in the book. They were the memorable characters in the grand drama of Durham life who shaped the lives of generations of Durham children. Many were not married; and in many cases, we were their children. The neighborhood understood: when "Miss Lily" retired, she was given a gift inscribed "From your children's mothers."

Think of writing a novel in which the central character is a school building—it is a story of a structure, to be sure, but it is also an institution: its leadership and staff; the women who taught there; the children who went there, learned there, and cared there; the neighborhood that founded it, defended it, and saved it. Great events swept through the school—two World Wars, a Great Depression, post-war prosperity, the civil rights era, the space age, the modernity of the 1980s and '90s.

For those of us who went there, the book triggers a flood of memories when the author mentions just a single incident. Anyone who went through the school (like Betsy Holloway and me and many others she interviewed in doing this book) carries memories of learning, of that first day of school when we discovered that boys went in one side and girls on the other. Who can ever forget Miss Gray's first grade class, filled with love and learning, as she told us the year-long story of the moon and "The Children of Light and the Children of Darkness," because she had wanted to be an actress and channeled all of her captivating skill into storytelling and improvisation.

And who can ever recover from Mrs. Pridgen's geography class (that's right, she was married, the book reminded me), where we sat very straight, and had our dirty fingernails inspected each day and were required before each class to raise our hand with a handkerchief in it (I still think of her even today when I sneeze without one). Miss Gray was love, creativity and inspiration; and Mrs. Pridgen was discipline, deportment, and thorough preparation. Miss Gray taught us to dream; Mrs. Pridgen to work.

Anyone touched by this history carries the memories of decorum, posture, and cleanliness, as well as the love of learning, into their adult lives. And who, once reminded by this book, can forget the smells, the clatter and the buzz of the cafeteria; or watching a non-athletic slip of a girl, Betty McBroom (as Betsy Holloway was then known) be the last one out playing dodge ball on the playground, so slender a target that even Kay Penny and Margaret Hannah, the super female athletes, just gave up trying to hit her with the ball. And I can still feel the embarrassment when I brought home an "S check" on a report card (as I once did for conduct), and the pride in pinning the safety patrol badge on our black sweaters and buckling the white web belt as emblems of office, and the joy I had when my father took the patrol on our annual trip to Washington and we all posed for a photo in front of Harry Truman's White House. Who can get over the excitement and the glorious freedom of a fire drill as we marched outside and heard a lecture by the "Singing Fire Chief," who taught us the value of cleaning up fire hazards in the home, before he sang "Mama's little baby loves shortnin' bread."

The great stage for events was the auditorium—where some proclaimed and some mumbled, but where we all became a student community. Time and again we marched two by two down its aisles for movies and plays, we child actors reciting our lines, surrounded by the green velvet curtain that Annie Watts Hill contributed in 1937, which lasted for possibly fifty years, and the "moving picture machine" that brought in the world from 1939 onward. At holidays like Thanksgiving, we sang "We gather together to ask the Lord's blessing," and at graduation, "J-U-N-E always spells Vaca-a-tion."

It was an institution devoted to producing "citizens of tomorrow." So we learned to stand up and recite in class, and thereby—without realizing it—learned to speak in public. The various clubs and activities, like collecting tin cans to help the war effort, or bringing food for the poor at Thanksgiving, taught us citizenship and community and to organize with our peers. It's all in the interviews, in the comments and the memories of the people Betsy Holloway interviewed.

And here was a school and a personality touched by literature and the stardust of Hollywood. Mrs. Pridgen, of all people in our town, was made famous by a barely disguised portrait of her written by Durham novelist Frances Gray Patton in 1954 called *Good Morning, Miss Dove*. A national bestseller—made into a film in 1955, with the title role played by the beautiful Jennifer Jones—it pictured a strict disciplinarian teacher who expects a great deal from the children she really loves, and who ends up earning the respect of the adults she once taught—and, ultimately, the whole town.

Frances Gray Patton also wrote a wonderful short story about an experience none of us would ever forget. It was inspired by an annual classroom project whose aim was to teach the glories of a balanced diet, while discouraging our appetite for junk food. Identical white rats were put into a glass cage: one rat was fed milk and cheese, and the other soft drinks and candy. Typically, the junk food-fed rat grew grey and sluggish, while the other one remained snow white and lively. The name of Mrs. Patton's story was "Grade 5B and the Well-Fed Rat," and in it the wrong rat died.

But the book is also a carefully researched history. With access to the Durham City School Board records, Betsy Holloway has written a fascinating history, too, of a neighborhood that wouldn't let its school die, and that always seemed to rally each succeeding generation of neighbors all through the century.

It has to be said that George Watts School was one of the premier white schools in a segregated city; and looking back, I cannot believe how innocent we were of the terrible burden of segregation on Durham's black community. But it was an innocent time for the children on the homefront of World War II, and the civil rights revolution that changed the South lay more than ten years ahead. Betsy Holloway does not neglect the twenty-five year history of desegregation, the eventual merger of George Watts and Walltown, just blocks away, the many threats to close the school as the student population dwindled, and the 1992 turning point when the school was targeted by the Board of Education for abandonment and possible demolition. The neighborhood rallied to save it once again, and convinced the Board to retain its familiar exterior, and gut the building entirely, and bring its interior up to code with modern plumbing and wiring and construction. In making its decision, the Board cited the 75th reunion that drew hundreds back to the school, its traditional racial balance (in 1974, a report had stated that the 233 students were divided into 124 whites and 109 non-whites, and that the PTA made it work because they were interested "first and foremost in the students"). The Board of Education report in 1992 also cited "a proud history" (from which the author takes her title) that included, the report continued, "a novel written about a former principal that was made into a major motion picture."

Think of how fitting the irony: the indomitable Mrs. Pridgen, who struck fear into every heart and who had died in 1989 at the age of ninety-two, was summoned in legend to help save the school she gave her life to.

I read this story with enormous pride. It is our story too, all of us who attended the school over its eighty-two-year history. The George Watts School we remember not only survives, it has flourished and been reborn as a modern school. In a time when there is a fascination with the new, and so much tearing down of old buildings, and trampling on memories, the neighbors in Trinity Park treasured their history, their roots, and their memories, and the common bond of our school that nurtured all the children and families who ever lived there.

Though this book is being published privately by the Friends of Watts Street School, and will be treasured by those of us who went there, Betsy Holloway has written a valuable book for American education nationally. I know the literature, and can testify that this is a rare "biography," if you will, of a single neighborhood school in a southern city.

This also is not a book mired in the hazy gauze of nostalgia. It is well researched, well interviewed, and well written. And it contains much for each generation to recall—the lists of faculty and the seventeen principals, the PTA presidents, the verses of the songs we sang as children, the thirty photographs and illustrations, and the memories we harbor of a long ago time.

Durham's deepest appreciation goes to our Betsy Holloway. As Durham moves into the twenty-first century, what greater gift could she leave her hometown than her three books: *Heaven For Beginners* about growing up in Durham; *Unfinished Heaven* about her teenage years at Carr Junior and Durham High Schools; and now her latest—about the history, teachers, and student generations of the George Watts School. With her indefatigable research, a lifetime of interviewing on her many trips home and a deft pen, the character of the school comes alive in all the many word pictures in this loving album for this century. We can thank Betsy Holloway for preserving and capturing this history in this bighearted and evocative book.

Eli N. Evans attended George Watts School from 1942-48. He is the author of The Provincials: A Personal History of Jews in the South.

*The equipment of the Watts Street building
will be the most modern available. . . .*

—Durham *Morning Herald*
1 October 1916

*This school is our oldest structure.
It has a proud history . . . .*

—Durham City School Board Minutes
17 June 1992

CHAPTER 1

The Building In Its Community

On 21 May 1915, Morehead School—the oldest school building in the Durham City system—was destroyed by a fire that started around 3:45 a.m. in one of the upper stories, and quickly spread to the rest of the building. According to that day's *Morning Herald* account, the fire lit up the entire business section of the city, so that Main Street appeared almost as light as if it were daytime. Despite the best efforts of firemen who had arrived quickly on the scene, the brick building was soon completely demolished. The newspaper reporter commented worriedly,

> Just what will be done with these [six hundred or so] children for the remaining month of the school year will be a problem that will trouble the school authorities this morning. All of the other school buildings are crowded, especially the grammar grades.

But when the City School Board met in a called emergency session that afternoon, Superintendent E. D. Pusey announced that arrangements had already been made for the Morehead children to attend afternoon sessions at Fuller School for the time remaining in the school year. (Fuller students would attend their school during the mornings.) The School Board decided immediately that Morehead School would be rebuilt on its present site.

In another part of town, though, discussions about the need for a school had for some time been taking place. Northwest of the city and adjacent to the eastern border of Trinity College lay a young, growing suburb that had been opened by the tobacco-wealthy businessman and developer Brodie Duke just after the turn of the century, when streetcar service had begun; known as Trinity Park, the popular new section was rapidly filling with houses built by Trinity professors along with administrators, businessmen, attorneys, and physicians. Mostly young, well-educated, and energetic, Trinity Park residents had already been gathering support for the construction of an elementary school in their area;

and a delegation from the area eagerly took advantage of the School Board's called session to present its request. Reporting on that meeting, the *Morning Herald* indicated the next day that

> some of the people in the Watts Street section of the town have talked to the members of the school board about erecting a building somewhere in the northwest section of the town. While this would be much more convenient for the children of that section of the city, the board did not feel that the city could afford to go into the additional expenditure of money for the construction of two buildings just at the present time.

Only seventy-eight elementary school-aged children lived in the section that would be served by a school on Watts Street, the City School Board Minutes noted in explanation of the Board's denial of the request. But this temporary rebuff did not end the story.

Trinity Park residents mustered their forces; and on 24 September 1915, reported the Minutes of the City Board of Education, a further approach was made:

> The committee representing the residents of the Watts Street section of the City appeared before the Board and presented a petition from the citizens of that section asking for a school building in their part of the City. Messrs. Salmon, Wannamaker, Glasson and Young spoke in behalf of the petitioners. Mr. [George W.] Watts, the Chairman, replied on behalf of the Board. Mr. [E. C.] Brooks moved that the Board erect a school building on the site of the old Morehead School, and an additional school building in northwest Durham, and that the Board proceed at once to secure estimates of the cost of the same and confer with the Board of Aldermen in reference to calling an election to vote bonds to cover the cost of the two school buildings. The motion was carried.

A week later, on 2 October 1915, the Board of Education voted to ask the Mayor and Board of Aldermen of the City of Durham to call a special election to vote on a bond issue of first, $75,000 for building the two new schools and second, an increase in the property tax of up to five cents, and fifteen cents on the poll. A few days later it was announced that the Board of Aldermen had voted to order the bond election as requested. On 14 December 1915 the election took place, and was carried by a large majority.

Now events moved quickly. Soon after the election, land between Watts and Gregson Streets, Urban and Dacian Avenues was purchased for nine thousand dollars. Charles Howard Lloyd of Harrisburg, Pennsylvania was employed as architect for the new building, with the proviso that he was to be assisted by Linthicum & Son of Durham. Already the name of George W. Watts, who years before had presented both the original (1895) and the new (1909) Watts Hospitals to the city, and who was then Chairman of the City School Board, was being suggested for the school; also mentioned as a possibility was the name of Col. W. T. Blackwell, who had been one of the first supporters of the public school system in Durham.

On 2 March 1916, plans for the new school—incorporating a modern warm air system for heating the building—were presented to the Board of Education, and were approved; construction began soon thereafter. Since the building had not been quite completed when school opened that September, the children who were newly zoned to go there attended classes for a few weeks at Fuller and at Durham High School (on Morris Street), as well as in a building erected on the Morehead property after the school burned.

As it turned out, the school was initially named for no one. George Watts objected so strongly to the proposal of the school's bearing his name that the idea was dropped, and the new facility became Watts Street School instead. It was not until several years after Watts's death that the idea of naming the school in his honor reappeared, and on 1 February 1929 the School Board acted. The *Durham Morning Herald* duly reported,

> In recognition of the services of George W. Watts, former chairman of the board of education, to the cause of public instruction in Durham, it was voted to change the name of the Watts Street School to the George Watts School.

But old habits die hard, and for many Durhamites the name of "Watts Street School" has clung to the school for over eighty years, despite the official change.

* * * * *

As Watts Street School opened, a Great War was taking place in Europe; but Durham was scarcely aware of it. The town was booming, with a dynamic industrial base: each day Erwin Cotton Mills used nearly 100 bales of cotton to produce wide sheeting, pillowcases, and linens; the Golden Belt plant, the largest cotton bag mill in the world, produced 2,000,000 assorted bags; and Durham Hosiery Mills, the largest hosiery concern in the world, produced 342,000 "Durable Durham" brand socks and hose. Dominating all else was the Golden Leaf: Durham manufacturers and exporters purchased 70,000,000 pounds of tobacco each year, most of it used to produce Bull Durham and Duke's Mixture tobaccos, along with several brands of cigarettes. Chesterfield cigarettes ("Like Getting Back Home for Thanksgiving—They *Satisfy*!") were selling at 10 for 5 cents.

In 1916 Durham had a swiftly-growing population, by that time in excess of 30,000; roads were macadamized or sand-clay (chiefly the latter), and a large number of area residents had electric lighting in their homes. (Christian & Harward,

Campus Scene, Trinity College, Durham, N. C.

Post card view of Trinity College, ca. 1915. Buildings are, Left to Right: Library, Dormitory, Craven Memorial Hall.

The Happy Home-makers, may have exaggerated slightly when they announced, "Most of Your Neighbors Have Done the Normal Thing and Purchased an Automatic Refrigerator. Have You?"; but certainly such household innovations were becoming popular.) The city had forty-six churches, a public library (at Five Points), nine banks—including one "colored" bank—and nine schools, six for white children and three for black. Trinity College, now twenty-four years resident in the city, had an attractive campus of 102 acres, twenty-four buildings, and holdings valued at $3,000,000; the school had 805 students and sixty-four teachers and officers during the 1916-17 school year. Optimism and action with regard to Durham's prospects were the order of the day: in August of 1916, a group of Durham boosters—which included R. L. Baldwin, Southgate Jones, and J. T. Salmon—had driven thirteen cars 105 miles through Person, Caswell, and Orange Counties to promote Durham's tobacco markets. The *Morning Herald* reported that the group had experienced a few punctured tires (these were more the rule than the exception in those early years of autos and dirt roads), but that these had been readily remedied.

Central to life in Durham was the downtown section, a busy, exciting place that bustled with enterprise and activity. As Watts Street School opened, P. T.

Elliott was offering for sale a Handsome Store Building, Now Occupied by the Durham Traction Company, in the Heart of North Carolina's Most Progressive City, for $25,000 (Terms to Suit Purchaser), with the down-to-earth reminder that "Durham Dirt Doubles Dollars." Most businesses had installed telephones (Haywood & Boone's Drug and Seed Store number was 3), and newspaper advertisements urged customers to telephone their orders. H. C. King announced that he had just received a Fresh Shipment of Horses and Mules, while B. C. Woodall, on Parrish Street, offered harness making and repairing, reminded customers that its buggy prices were now very attractive, and urged "Get Your Gun In Readiness For The Hunting Season!" Durham Vehicle and Harness proudly announced the sales of Maxwell Automobiles to a number of prominent persons in the area, including J. C. Dailey, J. C. Carrington, Dr. W. W. Olive, and J. E. Bowling. (The Maxwell had recently established the World's Motor NonStop Mileage Record: one auto had run continuously for forty-four days and nights—22,000 miles in all—without the motor having once been stopped.)

No longer was it necessary to hire a dressmaker or tailor to sew one's clothes, or to make them oneself at home: Durham proudly boasted a great variety of stores that sold ready-made clothing for men, women, and children. Rawls offered a complete line of apparel and supplies for babies, including carriage robes for $1.75 to $3.98, while Holloway & Belvin, on East Main Street, reminded customers that their fall footwear display was now complete ("The Styles are Correct—The Prices are Right.") Ladies' hats constituted a particularly resplendent part of fashion, and Smith-Albright, R. A. Baldwin and Sons, Mrs. E. C. Piper, and Mrs. Mamie Osborne had all held their fall displays early in September, proudly unveiling the newest millinery creations. Sneed-Markham-Taylor indicated modestly, "Our Advertisements are Small and Infrequent," observing that they aimed instead to provide their customers intelligent help in selecting wearing apparel (Men's Suits $10.00 to $25.00, Boys' Suits $3.00 to $8.50). Ellis Stone proclaimed, "This Store Has No Rival in Handsome Top Coats for Women," and reminded customers that "Now is the Time for the New Suits, New Top Coats, Dresses and Many Other New Things."

Entertainment was plentiful and varied. Lakewood Park, now ten years old and Durham's premier amusement park, had had an excellent summer, having opened late in May to the accompaniment of a Grand Display of Fireworks; this season a new $6000.00 Merry-Go-Round had joined the Roller Coaster, Bowling Alley, Skating Rink, and Natatorium. Alongside these attractions, the park offered a refreshment stand, Free Music, Free Dancing, and Ample Car Service on a 10-Minute Schedule, the latter courtesy of Durham Traction Company. The swimming pool supplied Bathing Suits, Clean Towels, and Private Dressing Rooms; and music was provided throughout the summer by a variety of groups, including the Durham Hosiery Mill Band and the Paris Orchestra (from the Paris Theatre in Durham).

Just beginning an exciting new season, by popular demand the Academy of Music had recently brought back the controversial smash hit *Birth of a Nation*, which had again played to packed houses. Early in October Andreas Dipple's Comic Opera, *The Lilac Domino*, was appearing at the Academy; Kronheimer's announced proudly that "The Beautiful and Talented Actresses Playing in *The Lilac Domino* will appear in our Garment Parlor on the Second Floor, Modeling the Fashions of Autumn." Every Durham lady was invited to attend the fashion show, but no men or children were allowed.

If you didn't wish to take the streetcar ride out to Lakewood Park, and the Academy of Music was a bit too rich for your purse, you could always go to the picture show. The Grand Theatre, which had just celebrated its fifth anniversary in Durham, was showing *The Devil at His Elbow*, starring Dorothy Green and Clifford Bruce ("See what rum and a woman can do to a big man!"); the Paris offered Billie Burke, Wearing Some Really Stunning Frocks, in *Gloria's Romance*, along with *The Grip of Evil* with Jackie Saunders and Roland Bottomley. (The Paris Orchestra, proclaimed the theatre, was a feature in itself, Every Afternoon and Evening Playing All the Latest Hits from Broadway.) The Strand was showing *The Haunted Woman* and *The Yellow Menace*, concluding the week on a somewhat happier note with June Caprice in *Little Miss Happiness*. Here and there an imaginative commentator would speculate that someday actors' and actresses' words would actually be heard in moving pictures; but in 1916 this prospect seemed remote at best.

Earlier in the year, Redpath Chautauqua Week, "The People's University," had come to Durham, featuring contralto Julia Claussen of the Chicago Grand Opera Company, the Parish Players, the Weatherwax Brothers Quartet, and the Schumann Quintet. (During the festivities, King's Drug Store offered a Chautauqua Special alongside its usual chocolate nut sundae, lemon freeze, and pineapple puff.) And as Watts Street School began its first year, the Durham County Fair was about to open, with its dozens of exhibits of livestock, homemade jams and pickles, and colorful, intricate quilts.

Music played an important part in Durham life. The two-story, Italianate Southern Conservatory of Music, at the corner of Main and Duke Streets, had begun its fall season, having announced earlier that Miss Clyde Kearns would again be associated with the Conservatory as a piano instructor. Not to be outdone, the Durham School of Music had indicated that Miss Helen Irwin of New York would head its Voice Department while Mrs. Alberta Wynne and Miss Daisy Robbins would have charge of the Piano Department. Meanwhile, the W. R. Murray Company at 114 East Main Street was advertising that it had just received a carload of Harvard and Dayton pianos, and that others would follow soon.

Post card view of the Orpheum–later the Rialto—Theatre (opened 1916) and the Malbourne Hotel (opened 1913), ca. 1925.

Building was taking place throughout the city. Thanks largely to the generosity of George W. Watts, the new First Presbyterian Church had recently been constructed on East Main Street, across from the elegant, solidly-constructed, three-year-old Malbourne Hotel; meanwhile, just a few steps away, the gleaming new Neoclassical courthouse and the much-anticipated Orpheum Theatre—across Main Street from each other—were almost completed, and would open officially in a month. The stately, Italianate Geer Building—on Main and Corcoran Streets, across from the Beaux Arts post office—had recently opened; harking back to the disastrous fire that had destroyed the site's previous occupant two years before, advertisements for the building reminded Durhamites that the building had Modern, Fireproof Offices For Rent. One of its suites was already occupied by Mrs. Lydia Anna Rosamon and her Studio of Expression, which offered comprehensive instruction in Physical Training, Rhythmical Exercises, Public Speaking, Reading, Recitation and Storytelling. Calvary Methodist Church had just been completed, as had Dr. N. D. Bitting's new house on Club Boulevard: Cary Lumber Company, D. C. May Painting, and J. A. Dennis, Electric Contractor took out newspaper advertisements proudly citing their contributions to the new structures.

9

Post card view of the Geer Building, Main and Corcoran Streets, ca. 1925.

Health was a major concern in 1916. Few effective treatments—and even fewer preventive measures—for disease were available; and what preventatives could be had were not utilized to full advantage: smallpox vaccination, for example, was still meeting with considerable resistance. Infections were greatly feared— and for good reason, as almost nothing could be done to halt their course. Diphtheria, rheumatic fever, scarlet fever, and even pellagra still struck with some frequency; and not many children escaped having mumps, measles, or chicken pox—or all three.

Watts Hospital, now seven years resident in its new location on Broad Street and Club Boulevard, had achieved acceptance among the population that had originally thought of hospitals as "a place you go to die." In September of 1916 the facility was crowded with eighty-five patients: every room was filled, and nurses were so busy that they were foregoing vacations. Nevertheless, many people continued to harbor distrust of hospitals and physicians, and home remedies of every kind—and of more or less effectiveness—abounded: BC Headache Remedy, a Durham product ("Never Fails to Cure! Never Dopes!"), was available at the druggist's in 5-cent, 10-cent, and 25-cent packages. An advertisement for Tanlac indicated jocularly that because so many formerly nervous and run-down men and women had regained their strength and put on weight thanks to this

Post card view of Watts Hospital, Broad Street and Club Boulevard, ca. 1910.

tonic, a clerk at Haywood & Boone Drug Store had proposed in jest that a "Durham Fat People's Club" should be formed.

Perhaps the one most common watchword for the time was Thrift. The Fidelity Bank headed an advertisement PLENTY OF FUNDS, and advised, "The time will come, young man, for you to march up the aisle with the dearest girl in the world beside you. When You Marry, though, you will want to have on hand a substantial bank account, for there is no affinity between love and poverty." One dollar would start you, the bank informed its readers, at four percent interest. The Merchants Bank struck a similar note: "Your Own Home is your castle. That's where you will take your bride and make your little nest. Begin now to save a part of your earnings and it won't seem any time until you have funds to buy some property and take your place as a substantial citizen." And the First National Bank, with Julian S. Carr as President, struck a metaphorical note with its reminder that Money held in its grasp the latchstring that opened the door between struggle and prosperity.

Although women were still a few years away from winning the right to vote, changes in the social climate were gradually taking place. Twenty years before, the bicycle—which had brought with it autonomy, freedom of movement, and sensible wearing apparel—had done much to liberate women from their restricted modes of behavior; and now a few daring females were already driving automobiles: at the time Watts Street School opened, in fact, suffragists Alice Burke and Nell Richardson were ending a ten thousand mile trip in their "Golden Flier," having given impassioned speeches publicizing women's suffrage in the cities and towns along the way. In Durham, while Five Points Drug Company still provided "private drinking booths for ladies," the *Morning Herald* was publishing a column called "Capable Women and What They Are Doing." (Kansas spinsters were organizing an Old Maids' Union, and Miss Marion duPont had been the first woman to ride astride at a New York horse show.) Meanwhile, international news brought word that while so many French men were away at war, females—who were working as cabdrivers, train conductors, chauffeurs, underground conductors, and butchers—had "practically taken possession of Paris." Although its full force would not be felt for many years, a tidal wave of change was in the making.

* * * * *

With Miss Jane Williams as Principal, Watts Street School first opened its doors on Monday, 2 October 1916. On the previous day, the *Morning Herald* had hailed the new facility with praise:

> The equipment of the Watts Street building will be the most modern available, and will compare favorably with that of the most recent school buildings of northern cities. The front part of the building is at present being graded and when finished will add greatly to the attractiveness of the place. Cement walks will be laid in the near future, while grass and flower beds will make the ground one of unusual artistic qualities.

A week later another, slightly cautionary note appeared:

> The playground is the most spacious of all the schools and with the removal of a few stumps, baseball and other athletic games can be played without interfering with the other pupils on the ground at the same time.

Two months later, Harrisburg architect C. Howard Lloyd wrote a detailed, two-page letter to the School Board regarding both Watts Street and Morehead schools, pointing out a large number of details needing correction: for example, all woodwork should have another coat of varnish; interior plaster work needed some repairs; several water closets were inoperative. However, he indicated, the contractor had used good materials in the construction of the buildings, and had followed specifications in every major particular. The buildings were sound in structure throughout.

Watts Street School, ca. 1918. Courtesy Durham County Library, Durham Historic Photographic Archives (DHPA).

Procedures and customs of instruction remained much the same for the first forty or so years of the school's existence. Boys entered school each morning by the left-hand front entrance, while girls used the right-hand entrance; the playground was similarly divided into boys' and girls' areas. Each classroom had a cloakroom at one end, concealed from view most of the time by a row of blackboard-covered doors. Pupils learned the Palmer Method of Penmanship—using steel pens and inkwells during the early years—and memorized poems, Bible verses, sometimes a Psalm or The Lord's Prayer, in their classrooms. The "platoon system," under which students had different teachers for different subjects, was in use from approximately 1922 until 1944; bells signaled the changing of classes. At one time a special acceleration program offered through Duke University gave pupils the chance to attend summer school before and after first grade, and then to be promoted from the upper section of the first grade to the lower section of the third.

The rapid growth of the Trinity Park neighborhood was bringing about a steady, and equally rapid, increase in Watts Street School's enrollment: only three years after the school's opening, the Board of Education recommended

13

1923-24   Sixth grade
Dorothy Newsom

History of the Sixth Grade

Drifting back in memory to the year of 1918, I can see a large number crowding into the school building to begin the year's work in their studies. Many of them were accompanied by their mothers to see that they were properly started off in their education.

For the first half of the year Miss Feraby was our teacher, she taught us how to write our name, and also our a, b, c's. From Christmas until the end of the year our teacher was Miss Trollinger.

In the second grade, when we had reading, those who read well would get a gold star, we had cards to put them on, and we all tried to get our cards full, before anyone else did. We all liked our teacher, Miss Lucille Pearce. We were all very glad when vacation came.

Beginning on this page and continuing through p. 16 is a sixth grade essay composed by Dorothy Newsom (later Dorothy Newsom Rankin) in 1924, tracing the history of her class at Watts Street School. Note the careful, precise handwriting, a product of the Palmer Method of Penmanship. Also note her recording of the "new platoon system," as well as the fact that after graduating from Watts Street School, her class would proceed directly to Durham High School (on Duke Street). Central Junior High (later Carr) would not open until 1926.

Three months later, we found it time to start to work again. We were glad to be with our friends again although we were sorry vacation was over. Miss Virginia Puckett made us enjoy the work so much more because she was so jolly and nice to us all.

We hated to leave her, even though we wanted Mrs. Williams for our teacher. We liked the fourth grade very much, except that the work was beginning to get harder.

Passing on to the fifth grade we were introduced to our new Platoon system. In this grade our school won several things, which our grade gladly helped as much as we could. It was during this year that we won the cup for thrift. And also several other banners for atheletics. The Girl Reserve organization started while we were in this grade. We had a teacher for each subject and we liked them very much.

We took up several new studies such as literature, civics, and also started to having phisical Culture every day.

In the sixth grade we did almost the same things as we did the year before. We were very sorry to lose the thrift cup but we were glad that our "sister school", North Durham, won it. In the Music Memory Contest we had second mention. Nine out of ten made perfect papers. In our geography class we made a map of North Carolina and wrote to the most important cities and then different members of the class wrote compositions and we put them on the map. We started the Red Cross Organization and in it, we made Christmas and Easter cards and sent them to the Oteen Hospital, and also did many other nice things. Nine months have passed since we started our work in the sixth grade, and now most of us find ourselves ~~rolling~~ headed toward the Durham High School.

enlarging the building. By 1923 the six grades contained a total of 110 boys and 109 girls; the expansion project was delayed, however, until 1927. During that year a major addition that contained classrooms and a gymnasium was built on the south side of the original building; at the same time ground-floor classrooms were converted to a cafeteria and the boiler room to a kitchen, while a new boiler room was added at the rear of the building. A decorative main entry was created at the southwest end of the building, replacing the smaller, less ornate entrance of the original structure.

During the sixty-five years following the 1927 addition, only relatively minor alternations in the building took place. Through both public school funding and PTA gifts, however, equipment continued to be added to the school on a regular basis. In 1929, for example, swings, slides, and "giant strides" were installed on the playground. By the end of the 1933-34 school year, noted Miss Lily Nelson Jones in her Principal's Annual Report for Standard Elementary Schools, the school had not only the playground equipment but also sand tables, a radio, an electric victrola, a mimeograph, and a nimeoscope [?]. A year later, Dr. and Mrs. James H. Cannon III presented to the school a silver loving cup in memory of their son Jimmy: this was to be awarded at graduation each year to the outstanding sixth grade boy. (The parallel award for girls, the Lily Nelson Jones Cup, was first awarded in 1946.) In 1937, the grounds were well drained and graded, and a piano was purchased for the gymnasium; in addition, thanks to the generosity of Annie Watts (Mrs. John Sprunt) Hill, the auditorium received a beautiful new curtain—heavy, moss-green velvet—for the stage. Two years later, the school acquired a Moving Picture Machine.

It was fortunate for the school that its addition had been completed in 1927; and it was remarkable that any equipment at all was added during the 1930s. Although the Depression caused Durham less suffering than was experienced by many other areas of the country (cigarettes, like movies, were among the few luxuries that many people could still afford), times became bleak enough that Durham citizens formed a Taxpayers League whose purpose was, as historian George Lougee explained in a *Durham Morning Herald* column from the vantage point of fifty years later, "to reduce unnecessary and excessive expenditure of public funds in the city and county, and reduce the tax rate to the lowest minimum without destroying the efficiency of government." This determined group slashed salaries of city and county employees (including the salaries of the judge and prosecuting attorney of Recorder's Court), terminated employees whose jobs were adjudged to be superfluous, and suspended activities of the city's recreation department. Hard times demanded hard solutions.

The city school system remained in operation throughout the Depression, though at times its survival seemed in doubt. Late in 1929 and again in April of 1930, the City Board of Education had to borrow $50,000 from the First National

Bank to pay salaries and other operating expenses. A month after taking out the second loan, the Board of Education found it necessary to suspend salary increases for teachers for the 1930-31 school year "on account of the existing economic conditions, and our own financial prospects." This was the first time that such action had become necessary since the teachers' salary schedule had been adopted about ten years before, and the Board optimistically hoped "that this suspension will be only temporary." Not only would the situation not be temporary, but things were about to get worse.

Other bank loans followed periodically; and when on 15 July 1931 the Superintendent announced to the Board the resignations of fifteen teachers, he suggested that the places of some of these teachers not be filled on account of the stringency of finances. Ten days later, twelve teachers were dropped from the City Schools' payroll. On 28 August 1931 the Board voted that teachers' contracts were to be prepared reflecting 10% reductions in salary for 1931-32: this reduction was applied to the salaries of all employees of the Board of Education, including administrative officers, teachers, and janitors. A similar action took place in August of 1932; and on 13 March 1933, following the examples of other cities, the Board of Education adopted a resolution

> that effective April 1, 1933, all contracts governing the employment of unmarried women in the City Schools of Durham shall include a provision automatically terminating such contract in the event of marriage while in the employ of the Durham City Schools.

This resolution was rescinded on 21 August 1933; but fiscal emergencies continued to arise, and for several more years the Board periodically found itself forced to take out bank loans to cover the school system's salaries and other operating expenses.

In April of 1933, a joint meeting of the City and County Boards of Education was called to consider the advisability of consolidating the city and county school systems, the first of many meetings that would take place during the next sixty years regarding this matter. On 15 May 1933, the General Assembly of North Carolina ratified "An Act to Promote Efficiency in the Organization and Economy in the Administration of the Public Schools of the State: To provide for the operation of a uniform system of schools in the whole of the State, for a term of eight months, without the levy of any ad valorem tax therefor." Five days later, the Durham City and County School Boards unanimously agreed that the State School Commission should be requested to retain the City Schools as a separate administrative unit. Members of the Boards believed that State appropriations to a consolidated system would be much less than to the two systems run separately;

in addition, the Boards could see no savings of money in operating the two systems as one.

In a special election on 8 August 1933, voters of the City of Durham approved a local tax of 20 cents per $100 property valuation real and personal, to preserve the nine months' school term by supplementing the State-allotted school fund, thus operating the Durham City Schools on a higher standard than that prescribed by the State. Marshall T. Spears, a Trinity Park resident who served as attorney for the City Board of Education, headed a committee of citizens whose job it was to publicize the election; subsequently he received a letter from the Board expressing appreciation for his great efforts in behalf of the schools. This choice by Durham citizens was regarded as an historic step towards achieving excellence in the city schools; but inevitably one of its results would be to increase the disparity between Durham's city and county school systems.

Still Durham—and Trinity Park—grew; and at George Watts School, enrollment continued to increase. Before the 1927 addition, a report by a City Planning Commission had advised firmly,

> [Watts Street] school has eight classrooms with 251 pupils enrolled in Grades 1 to 6. The school is well located in a rapidly growing neighborhood and is filled to capacity. The school is too small to be economical. The size of the plot should be considerably increased. Eight classrooms at least should be added and an ultimate capacity of 24 rooms planned.

On opening day 4 September 1929, 384 boys and girls reported for classes; just a few years later, in 1933-34, City Schools Superintendent W. Frank Warren reported that George Watts School had 460 pupils, an increase of eighteen over the preceding year.

By September of 1939, it had become necessary to set aside one complete room for the school's library, which by then contained more than thirteen hundred books. Cloakrooms and blackboards were removed in order to allow the construction of bookcases; magazine racks were placed about the room, and a library desk and chair were added. A year later, during the first year of C. C. Linneman's service as Principal, the cafeteria was completely renovated with the additions of a stainless steel counter and warming table, electric dishwasher, and new gas stove. An acoustical ceiling and new light fixtures were added, the tables were refinished, and the room was repainted.

In June of 1950, Mrs. Lorraine Pridgen, who had then been Principal of the school for five years, submitted her annual report to the State Department of Public Instruction in her usual meticulous detail. The school's enrollment had gradually increased since she had become Principal, from 287 in 1945 to 325 in

SPECIAL NOTICE!

Dear Boys and Girls,

Can you guess what we have at George Watts School which has new book-shelves, new tables and chairs, and some beautiful new books?--- A new library is just what it is, ready and waiting for use by boys and girls who like to read good books; boys and girls who want to look up something in encyclopedias; little boys and girls who like to look at books with pretty pictures, and teachers who need the books we have in our new library.

I shall be there to help you find what you want, and I hope you will help me keep it a pleasant, quiet place in which to spend many happy hours in "world of books."

Please come to me when you need to, for I shall always be glad to help you.

Sincerely yours,

Olive Faucette

Watts High Lights, September 1939.

1950. The entire inside of the building had been painted that year, Mrs. Pridgen reported proudly, with the exception of the cafeteria, which had been painted and repaired the preceding year. The classrooms had been painted a soft light green with a darker green trim; blackboards had been painted green, which Mrs. Pridgen noted approvingly was "most restful to eyes—a real asset"; and seven rooms had matching venetian blinds. The hallways were now beige with a darker rose trim. Special stress was being placed upon well-groomed grounds: during the previous year privet hedge had been planted on the north and south sides of the playground, and an exit lighting system had been installed for night meetings. The school now owned a phonograph and 118 records, while the library contained 1507 books.

Thanks to Durham author Frances Gray Patton, the community directed its attention with special fondness and interest toward George Watts School, and Mrs. Pridgen, for some ten years. In 1947, soon after her twin daughters had graduated from the school, Mrs. Patton published in *Ladies' Home Journal* a short story telling of a geography teacher, a veteran of several decades of teaching, who was a strict disciplinarian, but unfaltering in her love for the children in her care. Six years later Mrs. Patton's *Good Morning, Miss Dove*, a full-length novel inspired by the earlier story, became one of the best-selling books of the decade. Across the country readers were captivated by the redoubtable Miss Dove; Durhamites, delighted at such an accomplishment by one of their number, likewise hastened to read the book. Those who knew George Watts School and its principal quickly concluded that, allowing for a few minor liberties with facts, Miss Dove was an affectionate portrayal of Mrs. Pridgen. Although neither Mrs. Patton nor Mrs. Pridgen was ever known to comment publicly on this assumption, Durham's certainty of the identification continued to grow after a movie was produced starring Jennifer Jones as Miss Dove; and some forty years later, the Durham City Board of Education would refer with pride to the book and the film in listing its reasons for deciding to save and renovate George Watts School.

A few alterations to the building were made in 1965: "battleship linoleum" was installed on hall and cafeteria floors; four toilets were renovated; and new windows—glass block, replacing the old clear windows—were installed. (Steven T. Pulling, who produced a case study on the 1993 renovation and addition of the school, points out that many 1960s educators believed that clear classroom windows were distractions to learning.) Various exterior and interior equipment additions continued to be made from time to time; but after 1965 few if any major changes were made in the building for over twenty-five years, by which time George Watts School had long since embarked on a new path in education.

* * * * *

A PROUD HISTORY

On 17 May 1954, the Supreme Court handed down its historic decision in *Brown v. Board of Education of Topeka*. Justice Earl Warren read the ruling, which stated in part:

> We conclude, unanimously, that in the field of public education the doctrine of "separate but equal" has no place. Separate educational facilities are inherently unequal.

On the following day, the story occupied almost the entire front page of the *Durham Morning Herald*. Underneath a 2" high headline—SCHOOL SEGREGATION BANNED BY NATION'S SUPREME COURT—an article quoted Senator Richard Russell of Georgia as labeling the decision "a flagrant abuse of judicial power," adding that such decisions should be decided by the lawmakers, not by the courts. Governor Herman Talmadge of Georgia angrily complained that "the United States Supreme Court, by its decision today, has reduced our Constitution to a mere scrap of paper." In Raleigh, Governor William B. Umstead was quoted as saying that he was "terribly disappointed," but that he was reserving further comment until he had had a chance to read and study the decision.

In Durham, reactions were more restrained. School officials predicted that the adjustment could be made "without much hurt to the current school building program." Mayor E. J. Evans, calm and logical as always, reminded Durham citizens that

> the decision of the Supreme Court raises problems that will require the best thinking and the sincerest efforts of all the people of North Carolina. I believe this problem, like many others that we have faced in Durham, will find a solution that will work out to the best advantage of all concerned.

Dr. Alfonso Elder, President of what was then the North Carolina College for Negroes, commented,

> I believe that the Supreme Court's decision was wise and just. It is a decision that will pose many problems. I am confident, however, that the citizens of North Carolina, white and Negro, will work out the problems involved in a spirit of mutual understanding and good will.

Virtually all of the local educators who were interviewed for the *Durham Morning Herald* article felt that the decision was inevitable, wise, and fair.

It was over a year later that the Brown decision was mentioned in the City Board of Education minutes for the first time, as a letter was read from a group of black citizens who requested a hearing before the Board "to discuss the recent Supreme Court decision regarding racial segregation in the public schools." This request was granted; and on 11 July 1955, J. H. Wheeler—as spokesman of a delegation representing "various Negro groups"—read a prepared statement and presented a petition signed by 740 black citizens with reference to racial integration in the public schools. The Minutes indicate, neutrally, that "the Chairman thanked the group for its appearance and its interest in this subject."

During the seven years that ensued, Durham experienced "white flight" to the suburbs, numerous transfers of students from public to private schools, and occasional bomb threats. The City Board of Education, meanwhile, found itself awash in reassignment applications, denials, appeals, court orders, and a number of desegregation plans. Requests for reassignment were denied on many grounds, including the fact that the application was incomplete or was made on unauthorized forms, the fact that parents did not attend Board of Education meetings on the child's behalf, the fact that students lived closer to a predominantly black than to a predominantly white school, the fact of "poor academic preparedness and poor achievement records," the situation of overcrowded conditions at the school applied for, and the fact that the child was already assigned to the proper school for the area.

Compounding the already-imposing challenge of integrating the schools was the fact that educational facilities were "bulging at the seams," as a newspaper article reported in 1959, because the baby boomers were crowding in. (In 1958 the Board of Education assigned all sixth grade pupils attending George Watts School at the end of the 1957-58 term back to Watts for the seventh grade, because of overcrowded conditions at Carr Junior High.) New schools were built, but the numbers were such that—for example—many county students were denied admission to the city schools: on 1 August 1960 the Superintendent stated that nine schools designed as "overcrowded" during the past year were overcrowded again that year, and consequently were unable to accommodate any county pupils not already enrolled in city schools.

Lending further confusion and uncertainty to the decisions of whether, how, and when to integrate the schools—along with how to cope with overcrowding—was the perennial question of consolidating the city and county schools. In 1952, a number of discussions had taken place with regard to consolidation, but in August of that year a proposed plan was dropped. Again, in 1957, a study group was named to present a consolidation plan; but this proposal was defeated 5-1 at the polls. An awareness was growing that sooner or later the two systems would need to be consolidated; but for the time being other, more pressing problems took precedence.

Several years' delay ensued as a number of desegregation plans were presented to the U.S. District Court, and were rejected. Finally, however, in September of 1962 two black students were assigned to George Watts School; although these students apparently did not remain on the roll, by the middle of the 1960s the

23

school's racial barriers had lifted. City school faculties also integrated, with some difficulty—as the City School Board Minutes reported—in finding "teachers agreeing to teach pupils wholly or predominantly of another race."

Twelve years following its initial integration, and four years after busing had begun (to intense opposition) in order to achieve racial balance, George Watts School produced a Self-Study report in conjunction with the Cooperative Program in Elementary Education of the Southern Association of Colleges and Schools, pointing out in its Foreword that the school's student population had undergone a decade of dramatic alteration:

> Since the accreditation of George Watts School in April, 1963 by the Southern Association of Colleges and Schools, many changes have taken place. At that time, the membership consisted of 378 all white students. Most of these students came from upper-class business and professional families. Today the school is completely integrated and has a membership of 233. Of these 124 are white and 109 non-white.

Physically, the building remained essentially the same as it had been in 1963, stated the report, except that bathrooms for both boys and girls had been built on the second floor, and the library had been renovated.

The Self-Study Report further pointed out that parents of George Watts students had always shown great interest in the school and had actively participated in a strong Parent-Teacher Association; integration had not been a major problem here, because parents—interested first and foremost in the welfare of their children—had worked exceedingly well together to achieve their common aims. During that school year (1973-74), in fact, a black woman—Sarah Parrish—was serving as President of the PTA, the first black person to hold that office.

What was ominously apparent to everyone, although it was not strongly emphasized in the 1974 Self-Study Report, was that—paralleling enrollment changes in other city schools—the George Watts student population was steadily diminishing, having gone from 378 in 1963 to 233 in 1974. Certain amenities had disappeared: for example, the school did not have a cafeteria manager that year because of the small enrollment. Instead, a cook and two helpers were managing the cafeteria. The school's teachers were beginning to worry actively that the loss of too many students would result in the closing of the school; to avoid such action, George Watts eagerly took on special programs, such as the Hearing Impaired program, to attract students who would not otherwise have attended the school. Additionally, the curriculum was broadened by such means as establishing a working relationship with the Director of Music at the Watts Street Baptist Church, just across the street from the school, in order to provide a music program for the children. Two years later, minicourses—offered at the school once or twice a week by parents and other community volunteers—offered enrichment opportunities in music, French, woodworking, batik, creative writing, and dance. In a 1990 account of George Watts and Walltown schools, one teacher was quoted as commenting, "We were trying to have anything we could [during the 1970s] to keep our school from closing."

Their fear was well-founded. In both 1972 and 1973, mention had been made in the City School Board minutes that George Watts School might be closed. The subject came up for discussion again in 1974, at which time several residents of the school's neighborhood voiced objections to such action, pointing out that

> the school is a community center with racial balance, and that closing the school would cause additional parents to send their children to private schools.

A Board member responded, reasonably enough, that it was "difficult to defend keeping the same number of schools open when enrollment is one-third less than it was ten years ago."

School disturbances were beginning to occur throughout the country, and many Durham parents had become disturbed by what was happening in their own schools. Drugs and weapons were beginning to appear (such incidents involved primarily students, but City School Board minutes recorded the fact that one exasperated high school carpentry teacher had thrown a hammer at a particularly obstreperous pupil). Vulgar and profane language was becoming common; and security personnel were being hired, reported the Board minutes, "to prevent disruptions and insure adequate control of school situations at Durham High, Hillside, and Carr Junior High Schools." When a high school student delegation attended one School Board meeting in the early 1970s to present requests for rule changes at its school, discussion became so heated that Board members arose to leave the room—only to be stopped by students, who barred the doors to prevent their exit.

As troubled and unruly classroom situations prompted more "white flight" to the suburbs, a frustrated School Board found it necessary to keep revising attendance plans in order to comply with federal requirements. On 16 December 1974, reported the Board minutes,

> the Board indicated a desire to start with the neighborhood concept [in computer-generated plans for racial composition], but it was admonished by its attorney that if the Board's plan does not reach a certain ratio with reasonable percent of pupils in each school as determined by the federal court, then the federal court will impose a plan.

A pupil assignment plan submitted on 23 December 1974 provided that George Watts School would have 63% black students, 37% white.

A somber note was struck soon afterwards, when the School Board decided to close once-proud Carr Junior High, Home of the Bullpups, at the end of the 1974-75 school year: labeled "overcrowded" only sixteen years previously, Carr had for fifty years been the school that students attended following their graduation from George Watts School. Two months before the decision to close Carr was announced, four elementary schools—including George Watts—were targeted for consideration for closing; and teachers and parents alike wondered uneasily which elementary school would follow Carr's example.

But as events transpired, it was not George Watts School that was to be closed at that time, but the historically black Walltown School, only a few blocks away. Dating its operation at least from 1919 and perhaps earlier, Walltown had been fortunate in having a number of excellent, well-respected, long term teachers and principals who strongly emphasized learning and discipline; like George Watts, the school was strongly supported by its surrounding community. Although the Walltown situation was hotly debated in School Board meetings, at the end of the 1974-75 school year the school was closed. Ironically, both George Watts and Walltown schools were completely desegregated by that time; desegregation, in fact, was one of the reasons for closing the school since both races could now attend either school, and both school enrollments were dropping. Whereas for sixty years George Watts and Walltown schools had served as the centers of two distinct communities, now George Watts alone would become the educational center for both areas. In addition, the school would teach only Kindergarten through Grade 2, while Spaulding School would teach Grades 3-5. This division would continue for five years.

In November of 1974, a Lakewood Parents' Committee presented a distressed statement to the City School Board, clearly delineating the school system's Catch-22 dilemma:

> The Durham city school system would benefit by improving the racial balance within the schools. A desirable goal would be to maintain the same percentage for each racial group in each school in our system. An effort to achieve this is complicated by the declining enrollment in our schools.

> Between September of 1970 and October of 1974 the enrollment of blacks declined by only 8%, while during the same period the white enrollment declined by a much larger figure of 43%.

> The relatively high rate of withdrawal of whites from the system is continuing. To achieve the same racial percentages in each school would require complete redistricting every year. The disruptive effect of constant redistricting could be expected to accelerate the rate of decline in enrollment in our schools.

How the vicious circle could be interrupted, no one knew; and two years later, new desegregation plans were still being submitted. The school system, thought many disheartened Durhamites, was in disarray.

Despite the closing of Walltown and the combining of its student population with that of George Watts School, the future of the latter school remained uncertain. George Watts was, after all, an old school, occupying a considerably smaller amount of land than was currently advised in state educational regulations; and periodic discussions continued to take place regarding the possibility of closing the school. In the mid-1970s, in addition to the previously mentioned curriculum enhancements, an active, though low-key, public relations program went into effect—and continued for some fifteen years—to keep School Board members aware of the school, its traditions, and its strong place in the community. Members of the Board were frequently invited to attend such special events as Fall Festivals and spaghetti dinners; and a number of Board members visited the school during instructional hours, when the principal provided a school tour and perhaps highlighted some special effort such as the Title I reading center. At least once the City School Board held its regular meeting at George Watts School, where Principal Ruth Rogers introduced all the school's staff, and PTA President Dr. Curtis Eshelman informed the Board of the many past, present, and future activities of his organization. Gradually the school was assuming the "historic" mantle that would eventually prove to be its salvation.

* * * * *

In 1984, a graduate of George Watts School paid a nostalgic visit to the school, where she was surprised to discover how little had changed since she had graduated thirty-five years before. Classrooms still had the sectioned, blackboard covered doors at one end; each section had a doorknob that opened the cloakroom, which held a familiar array of galoshes, raincoats, and booksacks. Close to the teacher's desk hung large, colorful pull-down maps; and high on the walls, an alphabet in cursive script flowed gracefully around the room. The library held three decades worth of new books, including a number in such once-forbidden categories as comic books and Nancy Drew mysteries; still, *Alice in Wonderland*, *Black Beauty*, *The Secret Garden*, and many more old favorites remained. (Adding a contemporary note, a computer class was meeting in the library.) The auditorium still contained its twenty or so rows of pull-down wooden seats, bolted to the polished wooden floor; indeed, the room looked almost exactly as it had on that warm June day when the visitor—wearing a white organdy dress, and with her hair in fragile, unexpected curls—had walked down its aisle to accept her diploma from Mrs. Pridgen. The stage was still adorned with a heavy green velvet curtain, probably the same one that had been purchased by Annie Watts Hill in 1937; although the velvet had faded and the lining had deteriorated, the curtain remained whole.

Nevertheless, a few notable changes had taken place. Children now had separate entrances to the school by grade level, rather than by sex. Most of the subdued institutional green that had covered the hallway walls in 1948 had disappeared, having been replaced by bright reds and blues: apparently educators had discarded their former belief that children needed muted colors in order to be continuously soothed into good behavior and discipline, in favor of the more exciting theory that bright colors stimulated creative thought. The coveted Cannon and Jones silver loving cup awards for the "Outstanding Boy" and "Outstanding Girl" had been discontinued; and in fact the graduation exercises themselves, once such an important rite of passage, were no longer held at all.

In 1984, the same year as that visit, George Watts School was listed as a contributing building in the Trinity Historic District on the National Register of Historic Places. A Durham City Schools survey of that time indicated optimistically that "with repair and/or correcting of the items listed in the analysis this school will continue to provide a very functional learning environment for our children. . . ." Sixty-two physical deficiencies were listed, nineteen of them violations of state building codes. It would take ten years for these problems to be corrected.

But in September of 1989, a blow fell: a study by the State Department of Public Instruction recommended that because of its age, small size, and especially its many failures to meet State Building Codes, George Watts School should be closed. Fifty-four percent of the students would be reassigned to Powe Elementary, thirty-four percent to Club Boulevard, and twelve percent to a new elementary school; the existing building would be razed. Once more the school's supporters made themselves heard: Trinity Park residents, together with George Watts School alumni and local history buffs throughout the city, promptly joined forces in a vigorous protest against the closing, asking that the school be renovated and expanded instead. In December of 1989, school administrators recommended the renovation.

Meanwhile, acknowledging the importance of the now-historic school to a large number of Durham students, alumni, teachers, and parents, during the fall of 1987 the school's brand-new principal, Michael Courtney, had initiated a project that involved study of the school's history together with that of the Walltown School, whose student body had in 1975 been combined with the George Watts population. In cooperation with University of North Carolina graduate students, in February of 1990 George Watts students produced a study entitled *Coming Together: The Story of George Watts and Walltown Schools*. The book drew on interviews by community members, teachers, and former students of the two schools, together with school board minutes and other written documents.

In his Prologue to *Coming Together*, summarizing the state of George Watts School in May of 1989, Dr. Courtney described the school—at that time serving three hundred pupils—as a "community of cooperative learners," noting that "expectations are high." He cited such aspects of the school as a developmental, experiential science program; an Apple computer in each classroom; active reading and writing programs; the Drug Abuse Resistance Education Program; and the school's special links with Duke University and North Carolina Central University. Dr. Courtney concluded his introduction by observing, "Watts is an exciting place to be."

Using *Coming Together* as her source, Debra Frisher of the Durham Arts Council composed a play, *Watts A Wall?*, that featured all three hundred of the George Watts students, together with faculty members. The play was presented at Brogden Middle School, where it was filmed and sent to four foreign countries as part of the Durham Sister City Program. (In recognition of his efforts in behalf of the school, in March of 1990 Dr. Michael Courtney was named Wachovia Principal of the Year for the Durham City Schools.)

Despite growing recognition of George Watts School's historic status together with its significance to the community, for over two more years city school board members continued to harbor doubts about the feasibility of renovating the school. Again the City Board of Education was invited to hold its regular meeting (12 February 1992) at George Watts School, where Principal Delia Robinson welcomed Board members and presented a statement of the school's vision; Media Specialist Guthrie Moore showed slides of various instructional activities at Watts, and several PTA members presented an overview of current school projects.

It was perhaps not coincidental that while the School Board was still hesitating over a final decision as to the school's fate, on 17 May 1992 the George Watts PTA sponsored a 75th birthday celebration at the school, inviting anyone and everyone who had ever attended, taught at, or otherwise been associated with George Watts. Several hundred persons attended; and a month later, on 13 June 1992, a final decision was made by the Board of Education to preserve the existing facility, remodeling it to meet current building codes and school standards and constructing an addition to the north of the original building. The *Herald-Sun* reported that committees of parents had met for some eighty hours to detail the reasons why Watts should stay open, and commented,

> A groundswell of community sentiment toward the historic school led to an in-depth study on how it could be renovated and saved.

The addition was to be completed first, after which students would be transferred into that structure while the old building closed for renovation and repairs. A decades-old battle had been won.

The decision to retain and renovate George Watts School was actually one of the final decisions made by the City Board of Education before the long-discussed and planned-for merger of the Durham City and County Schools at last took place. Following earlier attempts at bringing together the two systems, in 1971 an election had been held proposing the merger of the city and the county schools, along with school bonds; both issues were defeated, sending a clear message attesting to Durhamites' unhappiness with the state of public education. When the City and County School Boards met together to discuss the recent action at the polls, the reasons presented for the defeat included 1) intense opposition to busing, 2) unwillingness of parents to support the merger if they didn't know where a child was to attend school, and 3) indecision as to how the money would be spent if the school systems were merged.

Though the subject of a school merger came up for discussion periodically through the following years, it was not until 1988 that a Merger Task Force Committee was established. Under the leadership of Dr. John H. Lucas, former principal of Hillside High School, the committee was assigned to assess the status of education, and to study and report on the best means of improving education for children in Durham's city and county schools. After three years of study and meetings, the committee recommended a merger of the two school systems; and finally, in April of 1991, a decision was made at the polls to accept the merger, which would officially take place on 1 July 1992. The name of the new system would be the Durham Public Schools.

Just before the merger took place, the City Board of Education included in its Minutes a justification of its decision to retain and renovate George Watts School:

> This school is our oldest structure. It has a proud history, including a novel written about a former principal that was made into a major motion picture. The students at this school recently produced a drama illustrating the history of this school and of the Walltown school.

> Its location, near Duke University, has fostered a number of interactions. These have been formal and informal, but always to the benefit of the students.

> It has been one of the better integrated schools, always maintaining a reasonable balance. It receives vigorous support from the parents and community.

> George Watts has a classic style of architecture, with generous use of brick, limestone, glass block and wrought iron. It looks like an urban school "ought to look."

One more nostalgic reunion took place at George Watts School before its appearance and function were transformed forever. On 31 July 1993, some two hundred residents of "the old neighborhood" gathered at the school for an afternoon picnic, reminiscences, and memories. Organized by Bill Kirkland, John Dominick, Jim Huckabee, Rhodney Reade, and Mike Troy, the reunion attracted former residents of the area bordered by Duke Street, Buchanan Boulevard, Club Boulevard and Demerius Street, from as far away as Connecticut and Texas; others who attended still lived in their neighborhood of forty years before. Rhodney Reade '49 recalled,

> They opened the building for us, and we were able to go inside and see it all again. And really, very little had changed since we had gone to school there. It was amazing how, when we walked inside, all the memories came back.

The returning George Watts alumni were informed of the building plan that would preserve the exterior facade of the building, while renovating the inside completely to comply with current educational and building code requirements.

This plan was carried out. A groundbreaking ceremony for the new north wing took place on 9 September 1993. The architects, Edwin Belk of Durham and the Robert/Stacy Group of Raleigh, had recognized that the 1916 George Watts School structure blended comfortably with its historic, mostly 1920s' surroundings, and had devoted considerable thought and time to designing the new addition, with the goal of making it aesthetically compatible with the existing building. The decision to locate the addition to the north of the school, rather than to the east, preserved the playground as well, even though the total amount of land in the school's site remained considerably smaller than the State Department of Public Instruction recommendation for an elementary school. The addition of the new north wing nearly doubled the square footage of the original structure.

Construction of the addition was completed in April, 1994: following their spring vacation, students moved into the new facility while demolition and renovation took place in the 1916 building. Since that structure's exterior surfaces and basic structure had been assessed as sound, its external appearance could remain the same. The interior, however, was gutted and completely rebuilt: plumbing, electrical and communication systems were replaced; stairwells were rebuilt; all windows, interior doors and hardware were replaced; and an elevator was installed. The renovation was finished in December of 1994; the entire project cost $4.4 million. George Watts School's 1916 building is now the oldest school building in Durham that still serves its original purpose.

The hard-won decision to retain, renovate, and add on to George Watts School pleased nearly everyone: it raised the school's profile in the community, and

31

Photographs of 1993-94 renovation of school. Courtesy John Satterfield.

infused a time-honored institution with new energy and new life. In 1995, John Satterfield '26 organized the Friends of Watts Street School, a support group made up of alumni and interested friends—the first such support group for a public school in Durham. During the three years of the group's existence, the Friends have provided funds to support programs for academically gifted, autistic, and behaviorally handicapped students, purchased North Carolina flags for classrooms, and helped to fund a teaching resource center as well as the new Wellness Center. The group sponsors field trips as well, and several members of the Friends serve as tutors for pupils who need help beyond that offered in the classrooms. The First Presbyterian Church and Duke University furnish tutors as well; and the University has publicly expressed its aim of supporting the health and stability of Trinity Park, together with several other neighborhoods close to the college campuses. And in May of 1996, George Watts School received an Architectural Conservation Award from the Historic Preservation Society of Durham for the preservation and renovation of the original building.

From its beginnings in 1916 in the middle of the Great War, through the Depression, World War II, and the changing winds of the 1970s, up through the preservation and renovation of its original structure in 1994, George Watts School has remained a steadfast tribute to determination and cooperative effort on the part of the Trinity Park neighborhood, alongside the larger community of Durham. With a lengthy tradition of dedication to excellence, as well as of marshaling community support to overcome obstacles, the school looks confidently toward a future of continued achievement.

George Watts School is a success story that endures.

The art of teaching is the art of assisting discovery.

—Mark van Doren

The faculty of George Watts School
believes that the teacher is the key
to the learning process.

—Self-Study Report,
George Watts School
April, 1974

For many years, education benefited greatly from the fact that teaching and nursing were the only professions that actively welcomed women into their ranks. Both professions thus received "the cream of the crop"—intelligent, conscientious young women who were eager to achieve, to see results, to make a difference. Dedicated to their calling, many teachers remained unmarried, pouring their intelligence, energy, and devotion into the children they taught.

"We were their emotional outlet," mused Eli Evans '48, nearly fifty years after his graduation from George Watts School.

"We were their children."

And in many cases, that was true.

CHAPTER 2

Principals and Teachers

One of the characteristics of George Watts School that has contributed most dramatically to the school's stability, continuity, and sense of tradition has been the longevity of its faculty. Many teachers taught at the school for ten, twenty years or more: Blanche Broadway, Helen Brown, Ida Cowan, Olive Faucette, Rhoda Kelley Hale, Mary Esther Harward, Susan Harward, Eunice Mattox, Agnes J. Moore, Mary D. Nesbitt, Virginia Sanders, and Elizabeth Walker were among this group. Elizabeth Gray taught first grade from 1919 until her retirement in 1958. "Miss Lily" Nelson Jones had taught penmanship at George Watts School for eight years prior to serving as principal for sixteen years; and Mrs. Lorraine Pridgen had been the school's geography teacher for over two decades before being appointed principal, a post she held for seventeen years.

One of the school's longest term teachers was Mary Esther (Williams) Harward, a 1930 graduate of George Watts School who subsequently graduated from

George Watts School teachers, ca. 1935. Courtesy Don Hester.
The oval inset photograph is of Lily Nelson Jones, Principal.

Ida Cowan

Annie W. Garrard

Mrs. W. L. Cridgen

Marie Tyler

Blanche Broadway

Helen M. Brown

Blanche Burke

Katharine Carter

Mary Esther (Williams) Harward, ca. 1970. Courtesy M. E. Harward.

Durham High and Meredith College. She began her teaching career in 1940 in the rural Bells School, between Chapel Hill and Apex; for the next four years she taught Music and Physical Education two days a week at Lakewood, and the other three days at Holloway Street School. "That was during the war," she recalled, "and I had to ride the bus a lot of the time: I would have to get on while it was still dark." In 1945 she asked for a grade, and was assigned to George Watts School: "I was anxious about it, because so many Duke professors had children there, and I wasn't sure I could please them." But please them she did, remaining at the school throughout the remainder of her teaching career, thirty-four years until her retirement in 1979. She reminisced, "It was always nice to see the children who attended the school, playing in the neighborhood," and added gratefully,

> I was so fortunate to stay at George Watts the whole time, especially when they began changing teachers around [during the 1970s].

Nancy Llewellyn Towe '48 reminisced about third grade with Mrs. Harward (then Miss Williams):

41

My mother had taught her French at Durham High, and was very fond of her because she had been such a wonderful student, so she and I had that bond from the beginning.

One day one of our classmates had a cough, and Miss Williams left us for a few minutes with our heads on our desks while she went to the teachers' lounge. Mary was coughing, and soon someone else began to cough; and by the time Miss Williams returned, we were *all* coughing. She was very upset with us; and she was such a gentle, sweet person that I went home absolutely heartbroken, and wept to my mother that I had let Miss Williams down.

She was the reason I became a teacher. When I went to Carolina and began my teacher training, I told them I wanted third grade; I spent three hours there, and went back and asked for sixth grade. I decided then and there that Miss Williams was a saint.

She was absolutely kind and gentle, and she never raised her voice; but she made it clear that if we did not learn those multiplication tables, we'd never see fourth grade!

Carrying on where her mother left off, Susan Harward graduated from George Watts School in 1960, from Durham High in 1966 and Meredith College in 1970; she began her teaching career at George Watts School in 1980, the year after her mother's retirement.

Although every child who attended George Watts School between the years of 1924 and 1962 emerged with clear memories of principals "Miss Lily" and/or Mrs. Pridgen, many have equally vivid memories of Elizabeth Gray, a native of Charlotte who taught first grade at the school for nearly forty years. Miss Gray had taught in Greenville and Asheville before she joined the George Watts faculty for the school year 1919-20; at that time she held a normal school diploma from the North Carolina College for Women, but subsequently she earned A.B. and A.M. degrees from Duke University. She assisted in Duke's program of teacher training from 1925 until her retirement in 1958; she also taught in Duke University's Summer School, and for the State Department of Public Instruction. Although she was frequently offered administrative positions in elementary education, she chose to remain in her classroom with the children she loved.

Margaret McCracken Allen '31 recalled Miss Gray and her classroom, confessing that

I really didn't want to go to school at all. I sat on Miss Gray's lap the whole year; she had lived with us, and I loved her dearly.

Her room was bright and cheerful, with long, child-sized tables, painted blue, with a flower on each end; and there were chairs to match.

PRINCIPALS AND TEACHERS

Dr. John Glasson '30 remembered her conscientious and exact teaching methods:

> She had very precise enunciation: she exaggerated the pronunciation of her words, and taught handwriting in the same precise way.

Several of Miss Gray's former students recalled their pride in belonging to one or more of her classroom clubs, among which were the Good Readers' Club, the Dramatics Club, and the Polite Club.

In a reminiscence that was included in *Welcome Back to the Neighborhood*, a souvenir booklet produced by Bill and Ann Kirkland for the 31 July 1993 reunion at the school, Susan Gray Ramos '50 commented,

> Miss Gray was the best first grade teacher anyone could have ever had. She gave me my love of reading and ability to spell anything because she drilled— and I do mean drilled—phonics into me.

Eli Evans '48, on the other hand, remembers her rich imagination:

> She told us stories about the Children of Darkness and the Children of Light, and we were just mesmerized. We would do *anything* to hear a story. If we misbehaved, all Miss Gray had to say to get us back into line was "Be quiet, children, or you won't have your story today."
>
> We would gather our chairs around her, and she would weave the story—colorful, mythic tales about princesses, and giants, and the light and dark sides of the moon—and she would act it out; each and every day she wove a spell. She was a teacher who was also an actress, using love and affection to draw us in, to teach us about imagination, creativity, the power of ideas, trust in one's own mind. We were riveted by her creations.
>
> When I came back to visit her ten years after I'd graduated from George Watts School, I told her she should write down the stories she'd told about the Children of Darkness and the Children of Light, and she laughed, and said she'd just made them all up as she went along.
>
> They were two sides of a coin: Mrs. Pridgen taught us to work, and Miss Gray taught us to dream.

* * * * *

Lily Nelson Jones, ca. 1935. Courtesy Hayes Clement and John Satterfield.

. . . each one of these children
will love and adore Miss Lillie
Jones as long as they live

—T. E. Allen, 1940
(in a letter published in
the *Durham Morning Herald*)

Among the seventeen principals who have served George Watts School, certainly one of the most beloved—and one of the longest to serve—was Miss Lily Nelson Jones. Many long-time Durhamites still remember the tiny, white-haired lady, an indefatiguable walker, who was known for her devoted, gentle approach to teaching, and for her loving guidance of the children who were in her care. Born 6 January 1873 in Cary, North Carolina, the young Lily Jones was first taught by Miss Alice Wilson (afterward Mrs. Walter Hines Page, wife of the American Ambassador to Great Britain), who at one time lived in the Jones home. Upon graduating from Cary Academy, Lily entered what was then the Greensboro Female College, from which she graduated with honors. After the deaths of her parents, she moved to Durham to live with her sister, Louise (Mrs. Joseph K.) Mason; she continued to live in the Mason household until her death on 19 May 1959.

```
QUOTATIONS FROM MISS LILY

"Good morning, children, are you any account today?"
"Don't bother about it, everything will be all right."
"If we have made mistakes they are mistakes of the mind and
    not of the heart."
"I am not afraid to trust my children anywhere if they are
    able to appreciate good music, good art, and beautiful
    things."
"Your conduct in two places tells what kind of a person you
    are: at the table and in a public place."
"My father used to say that anybody who would do that is so
    little he would rattle in a chigger's eye."
```

Quotations from "Miss Lily." *Watts High Lights*, May 1936. This issue of *WHL* was dedicated to Miss Lily.

"Miss Lily," as she was known throughout her career, taught in Durham's city school system for over thirty-five years. She began as a sixth grade teacher at Morehead School; after two years in that position, she transferred to Edgemont School where her fine penmanship was discovered, and she was made Supervisor of Writing at an annual salary of $750, teaching the Palmer Method of Penmanship to pupils in all white schools within the city. (During the early years of the century, students used steel pens that had to be frequently dipped into the inkwells on desk fronts.) Some sixty years after attending George Watts School, Frances Airheart Terry '37 reminisced fondly, "Miss Lily taught me how to write, and I still write large and plain." A 1912 letter of recommendation for the young teacher from W. D. Carmichael, who had served the previous five years as Superintendent of the Durham City Schools, commented that

> At the close of her first term as Supervisor [of Writing] our writing had improved one hundred percent, due entirely to her Supervision and direction.

> I feel perfectly justified in saying now that no City School in this country has a better writing Supervisor than she is. She has a way of being the best at what she does.

Dr. Carmichael concluded his letter by expressing his confidence that Miss Lily would measure up fully to his estimate of her, wherever she might be tried.

After serving several years as Supervisor of Writing, in 1919 Miss Lily became principal of North Durham School; in 1924 she was given Watts Street School to supervise as well. In September of 1929, she became principal of the recently-renamed George Watts School alone; and the initial issue of *Watts High Lights*,

Copy of a letter from Supt. W. F. Warren

DURHAM CITY SCHOOLS
Durham, N. C.

June 3, 1936.

To the Editors of the
"Watts High Lights",
Geo. W. Watts School,
Durham, N. C.

Dear Editors:

I understand that the next issue of the "Watts High Lights" will be dedicated to Miss Lily Jones, principal of the Geo. W. Watts School.

I know of no finer thing that could be done than to recognize a person who has given her life to the Durham City Schools. Miss Lily is loved and admired not only by the children, but by her co-workers. She is a woman of charming personality, enthusiastic over her work and, above all, possesses that happy quality of love for little children.

It is a pleasure for me, as Superintendent of the City Schools, to pay this tribute to Miss Lily.

Very truly yours,

(Signed)
W. F. Warren, Supt.

WFW: w

Letter from W. F. Warren, City Schools Superintendent. *Watts High Lights,* May 1936.

published in that month, marked the administrative change with a heartfelt tribute to the school's principal:

> We, the pupils and teachers of George Watts School, are sincerely grateful that you are now our all time principal. You are leading us forward always, and we are glad to be *on the way* with you.

Miss Lily remained principal of George Watts School until her retirement in 1940; a year before her retirement she was honored by being elected to membership in Delta Kappa, the national education fraternity. Even after retiring, she continued to direct writing and choral reading in the city schools until the close of the 1942-43 school year.

Students, parents, and teachers all loved Miss Lily. When a newspaper article featuring her and her teaching career appeared in 1936, the reporter began by commenting,

> No woman is better known or is more generally beloved than is Miss Lily N. Jones.

Following an admiring description of the principal's education, career, and professional accomplishments, the reporter concluded that

> her influence shall continue to be felt even after she has passed to the eternal reward that is the divine promise to all who love the Lord. For in every person who as a student imbibed so freely of her wise counsel and who absorbed the Christian traits that permeate her being and crown her hair of beautiful silver with a halo of loving service, she has a loyal disciple who is ready to hold aloft the torch she has so capably carried.

Carol Seeley Scott '32 remembers that Miss Lily made it a point to start off each child's school day pleasantly:

> At the head of the stairs inside the entrance door stood white-haired, sweet-faced Miss Lily Jones, our principal. Miss Lily knew all her students and greeted them by name, often asking about pets or family members. Miss Lily was beloved by all.
>
> In the hall behind her was a portable blackboard with the week's maxim on it in Miss Lily's beautiful handwriting. "Reputation is what men think you are; character is what God and the angels know you are," is one I remember.

Margaret McCracken Allen '31 remembered her similarly:

> Miss Lily seemed to love the children so much. She was always happy and gentle, and very bouncy: if you forgot your lunch money, she bounced in with a ticket for you.

May 31, 1940.

Dear Miss Lily,

We can never sufficiently express our appreciation for the years of service you have given to us and to our children. Nor can we repay you for this devotion. But we do want to tell you what an immeasurable satisfaction it has been to us as parents to know that our children were under your care; for you have always made our children, yours. This has meant to the little ones simply an extension of the affection and care which has surrounded them at home. But to us it has meant that our children were growing and developing under the loving guidance of one who really made their problems and interests her own; and who gave to them unstintingly of the wisdom of experience and the concern born of love for her children. And that to us was everything!

Beyond all this may we add that we, too, love you-- for yourself. We want you never to forget this fact. As a reminder we wish to present this small gift to "Our Miss Lily"--God bless her!

Your Children's Mothers

Letter to "Miss Lily" from "[her] children's mothers," on the occasion of her retirement in May 1940.

PRINCIPALS AND TEACHERS

Beverly Barge '41 recalls his former principal as "a short, rotund lady, very kind and gentle, who had white hair pulled back into a bun. I always saw her walking, no matter what the weather: she walked *everywhere*." And Dr. John Glasson '30 reminisced that "she was very kind and very fair, a motherly elderly person. As a child I had no fear of her."

Upon her retirement in 1940, Miss Lily was showered with gratitude and loving tributes—both public and private—from parents, former students, fellow teachers, and the community at large. Fourteen George Watts School teachers entertained in her honor at a luncheon at the Carolina Inn in Chapel Hill, presenting Miss Lily with a chain and pendant that bore her monogram on the front and the initials of each of her teachers on the back. Some 150 persons contributed to a fund that enabled the George Watts Parent-Teacher Association to purchase a diamond ring as a tangible symbol of appreciation, and of the loving regard in which the retiring principal was held; on presenting the ring to Miss Lily, Mrs. Wiley Forbus commented,

> There come times when mere words fail utterly to express our deepest feelings and emotions. This is one of them. We could never tell Miss Lily of our great and sincere appreciation for all she has done for our children. Each September we have sent them to the George Watts School with perfect confidence in her, and each June she has returned them to us, wiser, happier and healthier children. She is their second mother.

Accompanying the ring was a letter signed "Your Children's Mothers," a heartfelt expression of affection and gratitude.

In a letter published in the *Durham Morning Herald*, T. E. Allen explained that he was a parent of "six children who were fortunate enough to come under the influence and training of this Christian teacher," and continued,

> The debt of gratitude can never be paid in full for the patience, the encouragement, the high ideals inculcated upon each and every one more perfectly than the parents themselves were able to do. As a result each one of these children will love and adore Miss Lily Jones as long as they live.

One former student wrote her a letter that said, in part, "I do not see how anyone could be around you—even pass you on the street—and not feel better and be better." A parent wrote to her,

> In a rare way God has set eternity in your heart and it has shown daily in your life. Hundreds and thousands of children will always bear the imprint of the beauty of your heart and mind.

Another assured her,

> You have been one of my most valuable and heartening friends and I will love
> you dearly forever.

Miss Lily's retirement did not escape the notice of her former students: at the
Central Junior High School's closing chapel program that year, Marshall T.
Spears Jr. '38 presented his former principal with a corsage of forget-me-nots
and sweetheart roses, accompanied by a card reading "Love and Affection, Jr
High School Students." At Durham High School's graduation ceremony, students gave a standing ovation to Miss Lily along with Elementary School Supervisor Mrs. J. A. Robinson, in recognition of their combined ninety-nine years of
teaching in the public schools.

In addition to the formal and informal outpouring of praise and gratitude,
one final official tribute was offered in honor of Miss Lily's years of service. The
George Watts Parent-Teacher Association voted to sponsor a loving cup to be
awarded each year to "the best all-round girl finishing at the George Watts
School," as Claudia Powe Watkins, Chairman of the Lily Jones Cup Committee,
announced in a letter to the *Durham Morning Herald*. The award would parallel
the Cannon Memorial Cup, given by Dr. and Mrs. James Cannon in memory of
their son: at each graduation since 1934, the outstanding sixth grade boy had
been honored by having his name inscribed on the Cannon Cup. (Although
plans for the Lily Nelson Jones Cup award were announced at the time of Miss
Lily's retirement, apparently war metal shortages intervened; and it was not until
1946 that the cup was awarded for the first time.)

Perhaps one of the most striking compliments ever paid Miss Lily took place at
George Watts School's graduation exercises of 1948, when the school's former
principal returned to award the cup that had been named in her honor. Well
known for her strict and unbending demeanor, Mrs. Lorraine Pridgen had by
then been principal for three years; welcoming her seventy-three-year-old prede-
cessor with a respectful, admiring introduction, she deferred tenderly to Miss
Lily with every glance and gesture. Never having seen Mrs. Pridgen reveal such
emotion before, her pupils were stunned; many years afterward, one still remembered the occasion:

> When I saw the way Mrs. Pridgen treated her, I thought surely Miss Lily must
> be one of the most important people in the world.

And indeed, to her students and to everyone else who knew her, she was.

* * * * *

On the day I graduated from UNC, I came back to George Watts School to visit; and just by chance that was the day that Miss Gray was retiring, after nearly forty years of teaching first grade. I'd been talking with her for a few minutes when Mrs. Pridgen walked in. She offered her hand to Miss Gray and said, "Well, Elizabeth, it's been a privilege to work with you." And Miss Gray said, "For me also, Lorraine."

When Mrs. Pridgen left, Miss Gray said, "That is a great principal."
—Eli Evans '48

Mrs. Pridgen taught me geography. She was a little strict, but she did a good job.
—Warren Williams '33

No two teachers' styles could have differed more dramatically than did those of "Miss Lily" and the geography teacher who would succeed her as principal five years after her retirement, Mrs. Lorraine Pridgen. Many of her students held the same opinion of her as did a George Watts graduate of 1952, who commented tersely, "I was terrified of Mrs. Pridgen." A graduate of two decades earlier, who had studied geography with her, described her as

> the terrifying upper grades' geography teacher, who gave me a great deal of knowledge about geography and a great respect for authority.

Contrasting the real teacher with what she considered to be the "softened rendering" offered in Frances Gray Patton's *Good Morning, Miss Dove*, whose title character was rumored to have been based on Mrs. Pridgen, she observed,

> The real one demanded that her students stand up beside their desks to answer when called upon, and she did not mind shaming them, when she had daily inspection, for dirty fingernails or forgetting a clean handkerchief. She terrorized some children into learning geography. Others were too traumatized to learn very much.

Virtually everyone who knew Mrs. Pridgen would agree that she had a well-deserved reputation for strictness, and that she demanded order, neatness, and near-perfection from the pupils who came under her sway. During the years she

51

Lorraine Isley Pridgen, ca. 1960. Courtesy Mary Esther Harward.

served as principal, the worst punishment offered at George Watts School was being sentenced to spend the day in Mrs. Pridgen's office, huddled in a miserable heap under her cool, measured gaze; but a rare, quiet "Very good" from her was worth its weight in gold.

It had been in 1922, when Watts Street School was only six years old, that Lorraine Isley Pridgen had arrived in town to make Durham her home: although her arrival caused little stir at the time, its consequent influence on the school, its faculty, and three generations of students (and their parents) would be profound. A native of Burlington, North Carolina, Mrs. Pridgen was a poised, serious, conscientious young woman who had graduated from Trinity College in 1918, having first completed her practice teaching at Watts Street School under the supervision of one of the College's best-known educators, Dr. Eugene C. Brooks; she had then taught in Roanoke Rapids and Lexington for a few years before returning to Durham. On her arrival she began work at Trinity on a Master's degree in education (she was awarded that degree in 1930); as part of her course work she returned as an observer to Watts Street School, where "Miss Lily" Jones had just become principal. When one of the other teachers, Helen

Brown, contracted scarlet fever, Mrs. Pridgen taught in her stead. Soon afterward she accepted a permanent position as a teacher of geography and nature studies (the city schools had in 1922 instituted the platoon system of instruction, which provided a different teacher for each field of study).

Mrs. Pridgen had taught geography at Watts Street School for two decades when the school dropped the platoon structure to return to the traditional system; after the change she taught sixth grade for a year before, in 1945, being named principal of the school. She held that position for the next seventeen years, toward the end of which time she oversaw the education of a number of grandchildren of her early students, and welcomed the return of several of her former pupils when they were assigned to George Watts School from Duke to do their practice teaching. By the time Mrs. Pridgen retired in 1962, she had served as an educator for forty-five years, thirty-nine of them in the Durham City Schools.

By any judgment, she was exceptional. Upon her retirement, a *Durham Morning Herald* article quoted one of her former students as remarking,

> The children know exactly what they can expect of Mrs. Pridgen when they either do their duty or fail to do it. She's their security in an insecure world.

Extraordinarily self-disciplined herself, methodical and orderly in every task she tackled, she expected both the teachers and pupils who came within her sphere to be equally organized, neat, thorough, and self-controlled—and never to do less than their very best work. Mary Esther Harward '30, who taught at George Watts before, during, and after Mrs. Pridgen's term as Principal, recalls that

> her teachers knew that if they submitted an incorrect or incomplete report, they would be called to come to the school and make the correction in person.

And indeed, Mrs. Pridgen's own handwritten yearly reports to the State Department of Public Instruction are models of precision, neatness, and organization.

She required her students to enter her classroom in an orderly, quiet fashion, greeting her with "Good morning, Mrs. Pridgen" as she stood at the door. Pupils lined up each morning for inspections of hands, nails, and overall cleanliness; one of Mrs. Pridgen's strictest rules was that every child was required to have a clean handkerchief on his or her person each day. (Eli Evans '48 comments ruefully that "even now, I never sneeze without having a guilty feeling that I should have a clean handkerchief in my pocket.") Students stood beside their desks to answer questions in class; and when they walked in line to Music or Tiptoe Recess, they were required to remain quiet and proceed at a steady speed—but never dawdle or run.

Only the most intrepid, not to say reckless, students ever had the nerve to defy or disobey Mrs. Pridgen; and certainly almost no one was rash enough to play a practical joke in her classroom. But indelibly etched in the memory of John Satterfield '26 remains one rare exception,

> . . . the time Bill King asked everyone to drop a book at 10 a.m. Most everyone did; but when Mrs. Pridgen asked all who dropped books to raise their hands, Bill King did not raise his. When he was confronted about this, he said No, he did not drop a book: he dropped two.
>
> When Mrs. Pridgen finished lecturing us, you can bet your last dollar that there were no more books dropped in her room.

No other George Watts School alumni have volunteered instances of defiance of Mrs. Pridgen's strict rules, and indeed it seems likely that this was the only one that took place.

Parents were nearly as intimidated by this ramrod-straight, usually unsmiling Personage as were their children. Mothers who were summoned to a conference with Mrs. Pridgen suddenly became uncomfortably conscious of their grammar, and worried about whether their skirts were the proper length; nevertheless, George Watts School's principal always treated parents graciously and courteously—though firmly—as serious partners in the challenging, neverending work of shaping occasionally resistant clay into responsible, polite, conscientious citizens of tomorrow. (Most fathers pleaded work demands, travel, or any other reasonable excuse to avoid meeting with Mrs. Pridgen.)

When necessary, she made her own rules. Although she was routinely listed as Vice-President in the PTA list of officers, she commented rather bluntly in 1984,

> I rarely stayed for PTA meetings. I just told the mothers that I trusted them and knew they had the best interests of the school and the children at heart, and that I would leave so that they could feel free to discuss matters openly.

She had had a school to run, she pointed out; she didn't have time to go to such things.

Both as teacher and as principal, she was devoted to instilling proper behavior in her students in every possible circumstance. When pupils unwittingly applauded an American Indian presentation of religious music during an auditorium program, Mrs. Pridgen rose in offended dignity after the guests' departure to lecture soberly on the impropriety of such a reaction, driving firmly home once and for all the lesson that the only proper response to sacred music was absolute silence. At such times, when pupils had failed to live up to her high expectations, her sorrowful disappointment was even harder to bear than was her disapproval.

She never relinquished her authority, her sense of responsibility, her concern for her students' preparation for the examinations of life, no matter if they had long since left her sphere to become authorities and attain worldly success in their own chosen fields. When, in her later years, she suffered a hip fracture, she chose as her surgeon her former student, Dr. John Glasson '30. When he went in to visit her the evening before he was to perform her surgery, she fixed her firm gaze upon him from her hospital bed, and inquired, unsmiling, "John, do you know what you're doing?"

In her 1947 short story "The *Terrible* Miss Dove," Frances Gray Patton described a sixth grade graduation for which the girls were proudly arrayed in ruffled white organdy and the boys in white duck pants, composing "a group picture of purity"; her rendering could have been taken precisely from the exercises that took place for many years at George Watts School. After the graduation ceremony, wrote Mrs. Patton,

> [the students] went on to the wider world of junior high and, beyond that, to further realms of pleasure and pain.
>
> In the course of time they forgot much. They forgot dates and decimals and how to write business letters.
>
> But they never forgot Miss Dove.

And at George Watts, they never, ever forgot Mrs. Pridgen.

George Watts School is our school.
Let us be 100% for George Watts School.
May we never be guilty of disloyalty
in word, thought, or deed.

—Mary Eleanor Krummel, Editor
First issue of *Watts High Lights,*
September, 1929

Do you have the school spirit?
Do you have to be driven along before you do your work?
Are you grouchy with your teacher
if she keeps you in?
(Of course you shouldn't have to be kept in,
but if you are it is for your own good.)

Be sure and get the school spirit!

Editorial, *Watts High Lights,*
September, 1933

Some of the best times we had at the school were when the firemen came for fire drills: they'd always have several of the students jump out of the second-story windows into the fire nets.

But the best of all was when the teachers had to jump!

—John Glasson, '30

CHAPTER 3

SCHOOL LIFE

School life at George Watts has been rich and varied through the years, for the traditional "reading, writing, and arithmetic" curriculum has been supplemented by an impressive number and variety of extra activities. At various times during the school's first fifty years, those activities included Girl Reserves, Junior Red Cross, Brownies, Girl Scouts, Cub Scouts, Boy Scouts, Gray-Y, Safety Patrol, Audubon Club, baseball, basketball, soccer, track, *Watts High Lights*, Guardian Club, and Band. As the social climate underwent dramatic changes early in the 1970s, students began to attend programs on drug abuse, projects of the Durham Police Department and the Durham Junior Woman's Club. During the following decade and in some cases to the present day, the school has sponsored balloon launches, flea markets, spaghetti dinners, Scout Expositions, and the traditional Fall Festivals.

The tradition of supplementing the academic curriculum with extra activities began very early. During the school's first year, 1916-17, a few extracurricular pursuits were already in place: girls could join a sewing and crocheting club, while the boys had a basket-weaving club. In June of 1918, a number of Watts Street students participated in the Directed Home Garden project, a city school-wide endeavor that had been adopted by the School Board: four city teachers were appointed to oversee the project, the School Board funded expenses, and profits from sales of the produce were returned to the school system. (In the first

59

six months of the project, 485 Durham children had gardens with a total area of 92 acres. Expenses on the gardens amounted to $2326.69 exclusive of the teachers' salaries; receipts from the gardens amounted to $15,442.08.)

During the school's early years, thrift was a matter of perennial interest. In 1919, Superintendent Pusey reported to the School Board that a Savings Club had been organized in the City Schools, encouraging pupils to save money systematically by depositing it in one of the banks of the city. (Apparently some of the young savers did not regard this money as untouchable, for the Superintendent requested suggestions from Board members as to what steps principals and teachers could take in order to require children to keep deposits intact after they were made.) By 1930, Thrift Week was observed each year during the third week of January: the week included Budget Day, Make a Will Day, Life Insurance Day, and Own Your Home Day. Outside speakers visited the school to acquaint pupils with the principles of banking, investments, and loans. Students wrote essays on thrift, some of which were reprinted in *Watts High Lights*; they also created elaborate posters. (The *High Lights* reported that "Whitaker Young brought to Civics class a lovely poster illustrating the joy of banking," while fourth-grader Paul Gross made a poster that showed a squirrel saving nuts for the future: "The tree was his bank.") A debate took place in the Civics Society, with the topic "Resolved: that a person who spends his money as he gets it has a better time than the one who saves his money." With Allan Brown and Billy Davison speaking for the affirmative and Margaret Young and Billy Frazier for the negative, *Watts High Lights* reported, predictably: "The negative side won. We believe in saving."

George Washington's birthday was a particularly popular observance each year. Auditorium programs and plays presented highlights of Washington's life and accomplishments, while individual classes produced booklets, wrote essays for *Watts High Lights*, and sometimes learned the minuet. The entire year of 1932, which marked the 200th anniversary of Washington's birthday, was filled with special projects and events in observance of the anniversary; and on 22 February 1932, the upper grades of the school gathered in the auditorium to listen to the bicentennial program from the nation's capital over the school radio.

Fire Prevention Week, observed in October, always aroused much anticipation and excitement. Students presented playlets, wrote papers, and made posters in observance of the week (one second grade poster in 1929 showed a fire being ignited by wooden matches that were being gnawed by rats, and included the reminder to "put matches in a tin box"). For years pupils were given Clean-Up Campaign questionnaires that they were required to take home and fill out before houses were selected to be inspected by the Fire Department. (The questionnaires were designed to ensure that houses were neat and orderly, with no obvious fire hazards; and at least one mother always dreaded the quizzes acutely, because they included several inconvenient inquiries about piles of old maga-zines, which her basement held in abundance to entertain children on rainy days.) Students' essays on fire prevention were entered in competition with entries from other elementary school pupils; and in 1929 Louise Norris won the city-wide prize for the best sixth grade essay, the third year in a row that a George Watts School pupil had won first prize in this contest.

Usually several fire drills took place during Fire Prevention Week, their insistent, loud bells mobilizing students to energetic action with their tidings of study interruptions, and emptying the school of pupils and teachers in record times. Fire Chief Frank Bennett and several of his men visited the school annu-ally to clock pupils' and teachers' speed in vacating the building after the signal was given, and to demonstrate lifesaving procedures in the presence of fire. Dr. John Glasson '30 fondly recalls their visits:

> Some of the best times we had at the school were when the firemen came for fire drills, and they'd always have several of the students jump out of the sec-ond story windows into the fire nets.

> But the best of all was when the *teachers* had to jump!

After the courageous volunteers had landed safely in the nets, "Singing Fire Chief" Bennett invariably entertained teachers and children with his specialty, a lively vocal rendition of "Short'nin' Bread."

Other observances and celebrations abounded. Armistice Day was always marked by solemn, reverent auditorium programs that included speeches, poems, and prayer. After a Clean-Up Week in April, students observed Arbor Day by planting trees around the school building, and caring for them. Posters, con-tests, and talks by librarians marked Book Week, which was observed during the second week of November; a special auditorium program was held for the award-ing of recognition to those students who had completed a required number of books during the Summer Reading Program at the Durham Public Library. In 1930, pupils were asked to contribute a penny each to the Book Fund, the pur-pose of which was to increase the holdings of the George Watts Library; ten years later, the school's book collection had become large enough that the library was assigned a room of its own.

Throughout the 1920s and 1930s one of the highlights of the George Watts school year was the May Day festival, a blithe and colorful ceremony of youthful pantomime, music, and dance. Frequently directed by Physical Education Instructor Olive Brown, the event took place at El Toro Park (the old Durham Athletic Park); it included flag drills, Maypole dances and folk dances, and it involved all of the pupils in the Durham City Schools. Students wore costumes of foreign lands, or of characters from Mother Goose rhymes or fairy tales: Frances Airheart Terry '37 remembers that her mother once sewed leaves onto a bathing suit for her to wear.

For a month or two before the festivities, George Watts pupils busily practiced the dances that would be their school's contribution to the City Schools' presentation. A large crowd of parents and other spectators always attended the celebration; and the Superintendent of City Schools crowned the queen of the event, who was selected from the senior class of Durham High on the basis of scholarship, leadership, and beauty. Together with her maid of honor and a court of ten or more lovely girls in long, pastel-hued dresses of chiffon, organza, and lace, the queen reigned over all.

Helen Burnett Coppridge '40 recalled May Day festivities in vivid detail:

> One of my favorite recollections of grammar school days was our participation in the May Day Festival held at the old Durham Athletic Park. The queen and her court were selected from Durham High School students, and each girl held a large bouquet of red roses. I remember that one year Betsy Buchanan was queen, and Margaret Lawrence was in the court.
>
> Most schools did a Maypole, and we strove to have the prettiest wound pattern on the pole for George Watts School. This was accomplished by pulling strongly on our individual streamer while weaving in and out and dancing to the music as we circled the pole. I remember the music and the sequence of "one, two, three, hop, one, two, three, hop. . ." and holding our personal streamer over the heads of four fellow participants, then continuing the sequence while going under the next four, and so forth. George Watts always had the prettiest pattern on our poles!
>
> Each participating school also performed a dance. When I was in the sixth grade, our dance was a Hungarian Dance, and our mothers made our costumes. First, each student stencilled colorful flowers on white Indianhead material to be made into skirts. Red oilcloth was cut and sewn to be worn over our shoes (held in place by elastic bands) to look like red boots. We were told by numerous people who spoke to us as we left the park, that we had the prettiest costumes and the best dance on the program.

Mrs. Coppridge credited the excellence of the George Watts performance to "our physical education teacher, Mrs. Charlotte Allen, who worked with us patiently, diligently, and expected near perfection as we practiced, practiced, and practiced the Maypole Dance and the Hungarian Dance."

By 1941, the May Day festivities—hitherto devoted to such matters as Sun, Snowflakes, and Flowers—were beginning to reflect the darkening world. That year "Patriotism" became the theme: Rosa Mae Dean was crowned May Queen by

Photographs of May Day practices, ca. 1938. The photograph at the bottom of p. 66 may have been taken during an actual performance. Courtesy Louise Adkins and John Satterfield.

City School Superintendent W. F. Warren, in the guise of Uncle Sam. At the close of the ceremony, participants formed a United States flag across the field, and sang "God Bless America." Although the celebrations were discontinued in the early years of World War II, and did not resume after the war had ended, they still linger gracefully in the memories of those old enough to remember: shimmering, evanescent dreams of long ago.

Easter observances included parties, special editorials, verse, and illustrations in *Watts High Lights*, together with Easter egg hunts—and, of course, the observance of Easter Monday as a holiday, a custom unique to North Carolina. On Valentine's Day, each classroom held an elaborately decorated "mailbox" that contained all the class members' greetings to each other, distributed at an afternoon party that always included cupcakes (or frosted angel food squares) and tiny candy hearts bearing messages. But by far the most important celebration of the year was Christmas, when every room was decorated with a tiny Christmas tree, holly and poinsettias, and a Nativity scene. Children sang Christmas carols during auditorium programs, and many of the students participated in Professor W. P. Twaddell's annual Christmas carol service at the First Baptist Church. The Literary page of *Watts High Lights* included essays by pupils describing their

```
THE CHRISTMAS SLED

'Twas the day before Christmas
   and the clouds had turned gray
But poor little Bobby still had
   no use for his sleigh.
But Christmas morning when he
   opened his eyes,
What do you think he saw to his
   surprise?
Snow had covered the ground dur-
   ing the night,
And Bobby ran for his sled,
   filled with delight.
But a new one replaced the old,
   old sleigh,
And Bobby remembered
It was Christmas Day.

                  Sarah Gaddy   5B2
```

Watts High Lights, December 1938.

67

favorite pictures representing the Christmas story; the Poems section was filled with original verse about Christmas; and the All Around The World page described Christmas customs during the Middle Ages, in France, and in Wales. During the last afternoon before the school holidays began, the George Watts teachers held their own Christmas party at one of the teachers' homes, drawing names for gifts and honoring their principal as guest of honor.

(Christmas was decidedly the holiday of the majority; and during the school's first fifty years or so, little if any recognition was given to other traditions. Wryly recalling what was perhaps a subtle effort to assimilate him into the prevailing mode of thought, Eli Evans '48 remembered that he had once had to prepare a report on "The Meaning of Christmas"; to this day he recalls that the assignment was "extremely painful" for him, and that he received one of his few bad grades on that effort. In *The Provincials*, he relates the story of his having been assigned to play Joseph, "the number one boy's role," in the sixth grade Christmas pageant; when he declined the honor on the basis that this was too religious a role for him to play comfortably, his teacher solved the difficulty by casting him as King Herod's tax collector, a role that he played—wearing a bath towel as an Arab headdress—so broadly that he collected delighted applause and laughter in the middle of the touching exodus of Mary and Joseph to Bethlehem.)

* * * * *

In September of 1929, under the direction of Miss Blanche Burke (afterward Mrs. Frank G. Satterfield), George Watts School began its publication of *Watts High Lights*, a project that would bring to the school much praise, and many awards, during the years to come. (*Watts High Lights* was the second elementary school newspaper in the city: Miss Burke had initiated the first at North Durham School in 1927.)

Editor-in-Chief Mary Eleanor Krummel introduced the fledgling publication, which was typed and mimeographed:

> One project at George Watts School for 1929-1930 is to have a school newspaper. We hope to publish this paper each month. It is to be written by the pupils of the school under the supervision of Miss Lily Jones, Principal, and Miss Blanche Burke, Civics teacher.

> We appreciate the cooperation of the members of each grade and each department. Many of the articles reported in this issue are the result of work done in English classes during September.

> We believe that our newspaper will be the inspiration for better work in English, better school work in general, better attendance, and a fine school spirit.

Blanche Burke Satterfield, ca. 1938. Courtesy Louise Adkins and John Satterfield.

Editor Krummel concluded her editorial comment with a call for school spirit:

> George Watts School is our school. Let us be 100% for George Watts School.
> May we never be guilty of disloyalty in word, thought, or deed.

The initial issue of the *High Lights* noted that on the school's opening day that year, 4 September 1929, three hundred eighty-four boys and girls had been present. Four new teachers had joined the George Watts faculty, among them Miss Olive Brown, teacher of Physical Education. (Nearly seventy years later, Dr. John Glasson '30—who played on the soccer team that year—would recall fondly that "Miss Brown was a jewel of a person, and a greatly respected teacher.")

From the very beginning, *Watts High Lights* provided a showcase for students' essays, poems, book reviews, and artwork. Departments of the newspaper included News, Who's Who, Literary, Sports, Poems, All Around the World, and Jokes. The Literary Department of the first issue, edited by Frances Briggs, included a brief essay on James I by editor Briggs, together with autobiographical articles by Ruth Ramsay, Philip Corbin, and Mildred Whitaker, the last noting that "when I grow up I would like to graduate from Duke University and teach at George Watts School." Later issues that year contained essays on Robert E. Lee, Stonewall Jackson, Roman roads, and a Roman triumph. Perhaps because elementary school-age children tended to identify with a nation small in size, the newspaper always demonstrated a special fascination with Holland: children read books, gave reports, and wrote essays about the country. In January of 1934, John Carr Jr. vividly described Holland's windmills, dikes, canals, and tulip fields, and wrote, "In the [rural areas] the women and girls wear wooden shoes, very full skirts, white aprons, white caps with flaps on the sides, and waists with much embroidery on them." Class 4A2, dressed in Dutch costumes and wooden shoes, presented an auditorium program about Holland; and the *High Lights* frequently ran outline pictures of Dutch children for readers to color.

Along with listing the names of pupils who had made "A" on conduct and effort, or who had done especially good work in Spelling, Geography, Reading, Language, and Morning Work, the *High Lights* published a cornucopia of news, profiles, and other articles. One could find information about PTA elections and activities, plans for the school's participation in such city-wide events as the May Day celebration, and interviews with such prominent Durham citizens as businessman John Sprunt Hill, City Schools Superintendent W. F. Warren, and Mayor W. F. Carr. One issue of the newspaper included a profile of the school janitor, Willis Taylor. Students reported on their class excursions to Paschall's Bakery, Durham Ice Cream Company, and the Durham Public Library. Guest speakers and entertainers received generous coverage: when former George Watts students John, Alex, and Warren Williams brought their animal show to the school in 1939, the *High Lights* took special pride in describing the presentation in detail.

Pupils contributed to *Watts High Lights* frequent essays about their travels. Patricia Weeks wrote about seeing the king and queen of England during her trip to Washington, while Page Harris described her boat trip through the Panama Canal and Nancy Laprade recalled her visit to the London Zoo. From Mexico, Alexander "Sandy" Davison wrote about seeing herds of goats on mountainsides, being guarded by cowboys wearing large, embroidered straw hats. Nelson Stephens wrote feelingly about riding in a Peiping ricsha, while Harvie Branscomb sent letters to his schoolmates describing his experiences at the Berthold Otto Schule in Berlin, as well as the excitement of a German Christmas ("On every Christmas Eve in Germany everyone eats carp, a kind of fish which tasted something like an old rubber heel to me").

Teachers occasionally wrote for the *High Lights* as well: in September of 1929, Literature teacher Verdie Trollinger wrote about her first airplane ride—on a ten

FORMER STUDENTS EXHIBIT ANIMALS

John, Alex, and Warren Williams, former students at Watts School, presented a splendid animal show at the school on December 8. Goats, dogs, and monkeys performed difficult routines. A particularly good feature was the rope-walking dog.

In an interview with Alex following the performance, he said that it required anywhere from eight to twelve months to thoroughly train an animal to do a trick. He expressed the opinion that goats were the easiest animal to train and monkeys the hardest.

Alex gave his father, J. F. Williams, superintendent of buildings of the city schools, the credit for starting him and his brothers in their present work. "Training animals has been a hobby with us a long time and now we are commercializing it," he said.

He also said that he would advise anyone looking for a job to turn to the amusement business. "It is the best field for anyone right now with jobs so hard to find," he said.

Watts High Lights, December 1939.

passenger aircraft between Berlin and Dresden—and described her visit to Dresden's famed art gallery, where she saw and admired the Sistine Madonna. Olive Faucette, who taught fourth grade, wrote about her trip on the excursion train from Interlaken to the top of the Jungfrau, while sixth-grade teacher Helen Brown described, in fond and meticulous detail, her camping trip out west. Trips closer to home were reported just as conscientiously as ventures further afield: in November of 1931 the *High Lights* reported that Miss Olive Brown had spent the Thanksgiving holidays at her home in Wilmington; Miss Anne Garrard had traveled to Tallahassee, Florida; and Miss Helen Brown had gone to Chapel Hill. Miss Olive Faucette had stayed in Durham, but she had "enjoyed possum hunting."

In addition to students' essays and school events, the newspaper published news of Durham happenings of note, together with world news. Editorials frequently reminded pupils of their obligations to the school: an article in the *High Lights'* first issue noted that "Kindness" had been the watchword at George Watts School during September, and that "Self-reliance" would be the word for October. Several years later, an editorial inquired of its readers, "Do You Have Watts School Spirit?" and commented that [teachers and pupils] "seem united in loyalty to themselves and to the school." Students also had their attention directed to the community at large: one editorial announced with pride that George Watts students had exceeded their goal for contributions to the Community Chest, along with making generous contributions of food to the Salvation Army for Thanksgiving dinners for the needy. In December of 1937, Editor Caroline Lockhart urged students to support the campaign against tuberculosis by purchasing Christmas seals, while another editorial in that issue observed that

> if more people practiced kind thoughts, kind words, and kind deeds this would be a more Christ-like world and every day would seem like Christmas.

An editorial of October, 1937 reminded readers that Watts children were extremely fortunate to have had the opportunity of seeing a recent exhibit of some 150 pictures by recognized artists, and commented, "Many people come to Durham because of the reputation of the schools." The *High Lights* staff regularly exchanged their own newspaper with those from schools in other cities for comparison of format and content.

Sometimes the newspaper offered measured personal praise:

> Frank Warren was the first to understand borrowing in arithmetic in 3B2.

> Charles Boyd has become more reliable in the civics room during the past month.

Cover of *Watts High Lights.*

Cover of *Watts High Lights*.

Bobby Stapleford is very polite in holding the door open so that his grade can pass through quickly.

Jack Bright is helpful in the history room.

Bobby Gantt showed so much self-control during the month of October that we hardly knew him for the same boy.

Henry Leonard has developed promptness.

Helen Burnett is very reliable in her work as chairman of the program committee for the Robert E. Lee Club.

Banks Anderson is a clear thinker.

The newspaper also included news of exceptional alumni accomplishments, such as those of former Watts students Horace "Bones" McKinney and Bob Gantt, who were by then playing on the fabled 1940 Durham High School team that had just won the national high school basketball championship in Glens Falls, New York. When the *Durham Sun* sponsored a "Platform for Durham" contest in 1939, the *High Lights* noted, three former George Watts Students—John Carr, Elaine Childs, and Frances Powe—each won an award of five dollars for their prizewinning essays. During the previous year the newspaper had reported that Duke University had just awarded twenty-nine Phi Beta Kappa keys: four of the keys had gone to North Carolinians, and three of those four went to former George Watts pupils Mildred Patterson, Mary Eleanor Krummel, and Kendrick Few.

The *High Lights* included advertising as well as news: such firms as Rogers Drug Store, Seeman Printery, Ellis Stone, Christian Harward, Harvey's Cafeteria, and the Green Lantern Restaurant supported the newspaper by buying advertisements. The Ellis Stone ad for March, 1938 read "The Store That Dressed Your Grandmother, Your Mother, And Where You Shop For Finer Things To Wear." Later that year, Rogers Drug Company, Corner Mangum & Parrish Streets, noted in its ad, "We Fill Over 26,000 Prescriptions Annually."

By and large, the *High Lights* concentrated on school news, of which an impressive variety was published:

On September 19, Meriwether Wright brought a chamelon [*sic*] to school. It was a lovely green and when she put it on a teacher's skirt it turned brown.

The Polite Club of Miss Gray's first grade added many new names during the last period.

Charles Amis has to put on glasses. We are glad he found out in time to help his eyes.

Last month your reporter told you about Betsy Lawrence, who brought gold-fish to the sixth grade room. This month she is sorry to report that the goldfish have died. Betsy is planning to bring some more to school.

Progress notes abounded. A 1932 report from 3A2 indicated,

> We have begun to write in ink. It is rather hard on our clothes, but we do like to use the pens. We think we do rather neat work for beginners. Idrienne and Sammy have brought blotters for us to use.

And occasionally the newspaper offered a glimpse of the pain of learning, as when the 5B2 reporter announced glumly in 1933, "We have just started fractions. We find they are not so easy as we thought."

Students' health, or rather their illnesses and accidents, were always a matter of interest, and frequently were reported in some detail. During the 1930s the newspaper reported,

> Becky Barbee has had her tonsils removed. She is back at school after being absent a week. We are glad those old tonsils are out.

> We are glad that Bill Tiller is back after breaking his arm. He cannot write or play much, but we are glad to have him around.

> In Miss Broadway's room David Lockhart slipped out of his seat onto the floor. In Mrs. Pridgen's room when Clinton Pickett had finished reciting and was returning to his seat he missed his chair and hit the floor. We are happy to announce no bones were broken in either case.

> When Mary Smith was coming to school recently she slipped and broke her tooth and scratched her knee. We are very sorry to state it was a front, permanent tooth.

> A man hole [*sic*] fell on Jeana Davison's foot. We miss you, Jeana!

In February, 1938, the newspaper listed fourteen third grade students who had had measles that month. And "Durham Observes a Modern Miracle," surely one of the most dramatic accounts ever to be printed in the *High Lights*, recounted the story of a popular fourth grade boy who had suddenly and unaccountably lost his eyesight. After local physicians had examined him to no avail, his parents took the boy to see a specialist in New York. There he was hospitalized; but as his mother read to him one afternoon in his hospital room (the boy had at that point experienced seventeen days of unrelieved darkness), his eyesight mysteriously returned, just as suddenly as it had vanished.

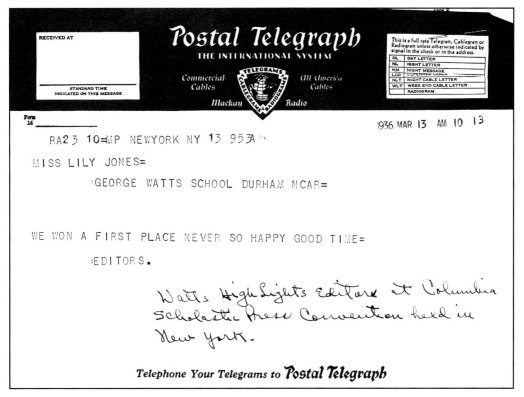

Telegram from *Watts High Lights* editors to Principal Lily Nelson Jones, telling of the newspaper's win at the CSPA in New York, 13 March 1936.

For the first four years of its existence, *Watts High Lights* won second place in the nationwide contest sponsored by the Columbia University Scholastic Press Association. Finally, in 1934, the Association awarded to the George Watts newspaper one of three first place prizes presented to elementary school newspapers in the nation: as a *Durham Morning Herald* article proudly pointed out, this marked "the first time that a grammar school south of the Mason-Dixon line [has] ever won that high honor." The *High Lights* maintained its first place position for at least five years (its ratings after 1939 are not known). Subsequently, Blanche Burke Satterfield received from the CSPA the coveted Gold Key Award for outstanding work in the school publication field: at that time, only eighty-nine persons throughout the nation had received the award, one of them being Miss Marguerite Herr, the *Hi-Rocket* advisor at Durham High School. Mrs. Satterfield continued as Advisor to the *Watts High Lights* until 1939, at which time Miss Blanche Broadway succeeded her.

Due to wartime paper shortages as well as the prevailing atmosphere of economy and self-denial, publication of *Watts High Lights* was discontinued during the 1942-43 school year. The newspaper resumed publication in October, 1946, shortly after Mrs. Pridgen became principal; but it is not known to have been published after about 1952, although at various times through the years the school has produced newsletters and other publications to acquaint students and parents with school and PTA activities. But during the years of its publication, *Watts High Lights* provided its readers with a colorful, ever-changing kaleidoscope of school life. And today the copies that remain recreate for the reader a simpler time, when children walked to school with little if any consciousness of possible dangers, when almost no one had heard of drugs, and when the exciting new technology of radio broadcasting transported listeners to front row seats at heart-stopping events around the world.

* * * * *

For most of its existence, George Watts School has been aided by a Parent-Teacher Association that has long been considered one of the most active organizations in town. The group was officially formed in January, 1920, only two months after the North Carolina Congress of Parents and Teachers had been formally organized in Charlotte. (Durham's first Parent-Teacher Association had been organized at Morehead School in October, 1919, although "Mothers' Clubs" had been functioning in the schools as early as 1914.) Forty-five persons became charter members of the Watts Street School group, electing Mrs. W. H. Glasson as the first president of the new organization.

During the school year 1924-25, every family at Watts Street School was represented in the membership of the PTA, although representation has varied during the seven decades since that time. From its beginning, the organization has provided equipment and supplies for the school beyond what was provided for in the budget: a *Durham Morning Herald* article of 9 October 1938 reported that the group had supplied a piano, a victrola, a loom for weaving, a mimeograph, playground equipment, pictures, and a visual education machine, and that it had "cooperated with the school librarian in making the library one of the finest in the city." It had also financed an art exhibition, as well as supplying needy children with food, clothes, glasses, and dental work. Programs at meetings during the 1930s included "The Importance of Mental Hygiene of the Pre-school Child" and "The Moral Effects of Failure." During the late 1930s, the PTA took advantage of the November Teachers' Day in Raleigh to sponsor as a fundraiser a "gymkhana" at Duke Park, offering pony rides, relay and sack races, archery and dart throwing, gypsy fortunetellers, a fishing pond, and hot dogs and hamburgers for all who participated.

Members of PTA and George Watts teachers in front of school, ca. 1938. Teachers (without hats) include, Left to Right: Annie John Williams. Lily Nelson Jones, Helen Brown, Olive Faucette Jenkins, Lorraine Isley Pridgen, Charlotte Allen, and Elizabeth Gray. Photograph courtesy Louise Adkins and John Satterfield. Identifications courtesy Helen Burnett Coppridge and other members of the Friends of Watts Street School.

Wartime saw the PTA helping with the metal and newspaper drives, as well as assisting in classrooms and on field trips; program topics during those years included "Wartime Care of Children," "Recreation in the Home," and "Psychology of the Problem Child." Late in the 1940s, the organization addressed the problem of a serious teacher shortage with a presentation entitled "Teachers—Past, Present, and Future." During the 1950s, the PTA bought duplicators, a portable public address system, and furnishings for the teachers' lounge, as well as supplying funds for the Safety Patrol and for the Christmas Party. (To illustrate the importance of fundraising events in the PTA budget, during the 1956-57 school year $261.50 in PTA funds came from dues, while $632.27 was raised at the Halloween party.) Program topics at PTA meetings during the 1950s included "What the Modern School Tries to Do for the Individual Child," "Hobbies, Their Origin and Role in Life," and "Schools Keep Us Free." The organization's Music Committee published a list of such upcoming events as a Four

Freshmen concert at Duke, and Lawrence Welk on television, "for those who like good pop music"; the committee also arranged musical entertainment for PTA meetings.

During the past three decades, the PTA has continued its long-time support of needy families and of Safety Patrol activities, sponsorship of fundraising events on behalf of the school, and provision of information to the community. In September of 1964, the group organized an "Outgrown Clothing Drive," the collections from which were donated to needy families in both the school and the community. The very successful "Halloween parties" of the 1950s have evolved into equally successful "Fall Festivals" that have included bake sales, fishing wells, ring tosses, music, puppet shows, a silent auction, and other attractions. As the school integrated during the late 1960s, the PTA strongly emphasized its first meeting each year as "Get Acquainted Night," in order that parents and teachers could come to know each other. When Walltown and George Watts Schools' pupil populations were combined in 1975, the PTA intensified its efforts in providing a hospitable welcome to the new students and parents, and in making information available to all. (Historically, the Watts PTA had taken a more assertive role in educational and administrative aspects of their school than had the Walltown organization; and this change in organizational activity was gradually accepted by the newer members.) By 1978, a PTA committee had seen to the renovation of the George Watts playground, providing a tire train, a balance form, three culvert tunnels, a climbing rope, and a basketball goal.

For nearly eighty years the PTA has worked in behalf of George Watts School, its students and its teachers. Much of the school's historic excellence must be credited to the parents who have listened carefully to the expressed needs of the school—and who have gone to extraordinary effort to supply those needs, and more.

* * * * *

One of the best-known and most-publicized school projects during the early years of George Watts School was Mrs. Pridgen's museum, an eclectic collection accumulated over several years that was housed across the hall from the geography classroom, and that had had its modest beginnings in a collection of seeds, stones, and leaves from the Durham area. Gradually the collection expanded to include items from other states as well as from foreign countries, and among its many offerings were an owl's foot, a set of squirrel's teeth, Japanese dolls, Cuban coconuts, Chinese tea and lichee nuts, and a Samoan grass skirt. The museum included an aquarium as well, for which the children contributed plants, fish, and fish food. Students who did particularly good work were occasionally allowed to look through the old stereoscope in the room.

AQUARIUM LOOKS GOOD

The aquarium in the science room is beginning to develop into a center of interest. Mrs. Pridgen says that it is there to let the children see how animals and plants grow in water.

Many children have brought things for it. Sita Hamilton, Gladys Noell, Beverley Barge, and Jean Satterwhite, brought plants. Patsy Crum, Martha Rose Meyers, and Beverley Barge brought fish. The fish food was brought by Patsy Crum and Pauline Locklear.

The third grade is particularly interested in the aquarium at the present since they are studying animals and plants.

Watts High Lights, September 1939.

For a decade or more during the 1930s and 1940s, each Wednesday was known as "Society Day" in the Civics Department. Under the direction of Mrs. Blanche Burke Satterfield, officers were elected twice a year, and programs honored the birthdays of famous men with talks, plays, music, and art. Public questions were debated, and such observances as Thrift Week and Red Cross Week were given special emphasis. Students received practice in public speaking, and a newspaper article reporting on the civic society indicated proudly that the project encouraged "development of reliability, self-reliance, self-control, good workmanship, cooperation and courtesy." Carol Seeley Scott '32 recalls,

> On Wednesdays in the upper grades in civics class we had what we called "Soci-
> ety" [in the auditorium]. This consisted of programs planned and put on by
> members of the class, with the class president presiding and the secretary tak-
> ing notes for the minutes to be read the next week. Throughout the year we
> took turns reading, singing, playing musical selections, reciting poems. We
> were learning how to appear in front of an audience with confidence, and the
> fundamentals of group organization, and didn't realize it.

Always encouraged to become aware of current world events, on 12 May 1937
Watts pupils listened to a radio address given by King George VI on his corona-
tion day. (The precise events that had resulted in the new monarch's accession
to the throne remained cloudy in most young minds of the radio audience.)
Years before, as he walked to school, young John Glasson '30 had heard more
informally of another remarkable event from a classmate, Osborne Stallings: "A
fellow named Line-berg has just flown across the Atlantic Ocean."

Music was popular in all forms at George Watts School, and much effort was
expended to insure that students would develop a knowledge and an appreciation of this study. During the 1930s, the upper grades and their teachers gathered in the auditorium on Friday afternoons to listen to the Walter Damrosch
orchestral program for schoolchildren over the school's radio. Carol Seeley
Scott '32 remembers that

> with accompanying workbooks we learned to identify each of the instruments
> in an orchestra by sight and sound, and [we] became familiar with many pieces
> of classical orchestral music.

Many of the most popular auditorium programs were musical in nature: one featured vocalist C. S. Hooper, then a student at Central Junior High School, who
presented a varied selection of classical and popular songs. Duke's Director of
Choral Music, J. Foster Barnes, and Mrs. Barnes—whose daughter Barbara
edited *Watts High Lights* as a sixth-grader—visited to perform a musical program
together. The North Carolina Symphony Orchestra contributed many enriching
programs through the years. At times during the 1930s, the school had its own
small orchestra: one, in 1939, featured Sammy Gantt playing baritone horn, Dou-
glas Ausbon the clarinet, and Robert White the drum. On occasion Watts had
harmonica and piccolo bands, together with Glee Clubs of fifty or so members.

But perhaps many George Watts graduates' most vivid musical memories are
the simpler ones: singing "Beautiful Dreamer," "Funiculi, Funicula" and "Stout-
hearted Men" in fourth grade music, joining in "We Gather Together" to open
the Thanksgiving auditorium program, caroling "O Come, All Ye Faithful" and
"Joy to the World" during the Christmas season. And no graduation exercise
would have been complete without a spirited rendition of "The Vacation Song":

SCHOOL LIFE

Is there anything you want to know? Just ask us, we can tell,
We've studied hard for nine long months, and we know our lessons well,
But now we're looking for the time when we can have some fun,
For J-U-N-E always spells VA-CA-TION!

* * * * *

Durham High may be good, Duke and Carolina better,
but watch out for Watts Street!

—School cheer, 1930s

Anticipating some of the vigorous interests of Durham High and Duke, sports have always played a significant part in George Watts's school life. During the early years, soccer was one of the most popular sports for boys. Recalling that time, Dr. John Glasson '30 reminisced,

> I played soccer for Watts Street School: we kicked the ball between two pine trees. Once in a while we'd get adventurous and play E. K. Powe, which always had some real ruffians on its team.

In September of 1929, John Cheek, Sports Editor of the *Watts High Lights*, announced that soccer had been the school's best sport that year, and that Miss [Olive] Brown was taking charge of the team. In 1931, thirty-one boys went out for soccer, including Horace [later "Bones"] McKinney,. M. B. Fowler, Jack Markham, and Bobby Gantt; out of those, twenty-five were chosen for the school soccer team. That team won the soccer championship of the west side of Durham, and nearly won the city championship: George Watts tied Edgemont for two games before being defeated by that always-formidable team in the third.

Other than soccer, basketball was popular both between classes within the school, and against other schools. Boys played touch football (often the game was, as Eli Evans '48 recalled, "incredibly rough"). For a number of years George Watts students participated in the annual grammar school track meet that was held at Duke University Stadium. At recess and occasionally in intramural games, both boys and girls played softball, kick ball, and dodge ball. One non-athletic female graduate of George Watts's Class of '48 recalls fondly that the greatest sports triumph of her life took place in a dodge ball game during recess, when she somehow managed to stay alone in the ring to dodge ten powerful throws by the two best athletes of the sixth grade, while the rest of her class-mates—stunned by this unexpected accomplishment by the smallest, least coor-dinated of their number—stood by and cheered.

Not all of the activities at recess were organized. Yoyos appeared frequently, usually in the springtime, and the more gifted twirlers held sway with Walk-the-Dog, Round-the-World, and other showy maneuvers. Students occasionally brought their Brownie Hawkeye cameras to record their classmates and teachers for posterity. One graduate remembers that late in the 1940s a passion for horses gripped several of the fifth and sixth grade girls, who took to spending their free moments cantering, whinnying, and galloping around the playground. Members of Mrs. Zollicoffer's Girl Scout Troop recited a lengthy story of the deeds of "Sticky-sticky-stombone" to whoever would listen; and sometimes girls practiced the tango, waltz, and foxtrot steps that they had learned in Mr. Satterfield's dance class the week before. (The boys did not seem interested in joining this activity.) When blond, petite Grace Hess joined the fifth grade in 1946, she brought to her classmates a passion for turning cartwheels and handsprings; and soon girls began to beg their mothers for underwear that matched their dresses so that when they performed their gymnastic feats—which somehow never looked as light and effortless as Grace's—their white underpants would not be revealed to the eyes of curious, snickering male onlookers. The boys, when not engaged in football, sometimes studied Johnson Smith catalogues with their offerings of Whoopee Cushions, Dribble Glasses, and Rubber Dog Doo. They also entertained each other with contraband copies of the *National Geographic*, which could be depended upon to offer photographs of Samoan women, bare to the waist. (These diversions never lasted long, as teachers always became quickly alert to the sight of a group of boys giggling together; and the magazine's owner usually found himself hustled unceremoniously to the office, where he spent the remainder of the day hunched miserably in a desk, his shamed gaze meeting only the icy stare of Mrs. Pridgen when he dared to raise his eyes from the floor.)

One of the more impressive honors that could be won by George Watts boys was membership in the Safety Patrol, whose responsibility it was to help students cross streets safely on the way to and from school. The idea for the patrols had come about in 1926, after a child had been hit in front of E. K. Powe School; subsequently, merchants in that area approached the Police Department to ask that some action be taken to insure schoolchildren's safety. Police joined forces with the City Recreation Department to start a program in which students would act as crosswalk guards, and the idea became popular with other schools throughout the city and county. Sometimes the Safety Patrol acted in capacities other than that of directing traffic: the October, 1929 *Watts High Lights* commented admiringly,

> We wish to congratulate the Safety Patrol boys in their success as hall monitors. We have noticed a great improvement in conduct as we march. These boys hold positions of trust, and we are glad that the students of George Watts School respect and obey them.

George Watts Safety Patrol, 1946. Photograph and identifications courtesy Tommy Hunt. Members include, Left to Right, Walter Barge, Tommy Hunt, Earl Farlow, Rufus Hackney, Bill Aldridge, Bob Brunson, Sterling Brockwell, Don Conklin, Charles Green, Carl Lloyd Cooper, Gordon Ward, Barry Fogel.

Although most of the patrol members came from the sixth grade, a number of fifth and fourth grade boys were also included.

Safety Patrol members wore dark blue sweaters with identifying Patrol badges and white bands across the sweater, dark blue pants, and white caps. One former member reminisced, "It was a really big thing, being on the Safety Patrol—having a uniform, and power." (Probably Patrolers did not actually have the authority to stop a car, but their position commanded much respect.) The organization began performing drills in 1932; several inspections took place each year at the City Armory, and in 1946, 1952, and a number of years following, the George Watts group received highest honors, thereby winning the T. A. Winder Award—a United States flag, with holder. Occasionally the Patrol took trips to points of interest within the state, but the undisputed high point of the year was the spring trip to Washington, D.C. There the boys visited the FBI, the mint, the Smithsonian Institute, the Capitol, and the Lincoln and Jefferson Memorials, and joined other Patrolers from across the nation in a march down Constitution Avenue, where they were reviewed by the President and other government officials.

```
SAFETY PATROLS

Safety Patrols of George Watts
    School
Have always tried to keep the
    rule.
Day by Day our corners are kept
By Safety Patrols who watch
    their step.
Not an accident has happened for
    many a year.
The Safety Patrol was founded
    here.
We hope to keep our record clean
    here and now and the years
    between,
The time when we will be in a
    band and help to rule and
    govern our land.
      E. K. Powe and Bobby Gantt
```

Watts High Lights, April 1934.

Stung by accusations of being discriminatory, Safety Patrols began admitting girls to their ranks during the 1970s; but eventually the groups came under fire again for their grade requirements, their "militarism," and the inspections. Durham's county schools dropped the program in 1989, and city schools soon followed suit. Still, the image of clean-cut boys in crisp uniforms, standing tall and proud as they helped small, awestruck first and second graders across streets, remains pleasantly in the memories of many George Watts graduates; and for many years the Safety Patrol played a major role in the lives of those boys who were honored by being allowed to participate in its program.

During George Watts's first eleven years, students carried their lunches to school; but as a part of the 1927 addition, the school acquired a cafeteria. The new facility was located in the basement, which was actually only half a floor beneath ground level, so that when pupils looked out the windows that were near the ceiling, they could gaze at the sky, with an occasional tree top for variety. Meat loaf, boiled carrots, mashed potatoes, and Jello appeared regularly on the cafeteria line. Frances Airheart Terry '37, whose years at George Watts School coincided with the worst years of the Depression, recalls that "they served macaroni and cheese so often that it wasn't until years later that I could eat it again." Another frequent menu offering during those years, she comments, was an item of such uncertain provenance that the students christened it "dishwater soup" (Carol Seeley Scott '32 remembers the name as "dishwater and soap").

```
CLEAN PLATE CLUB

     The following children in
3B2 have been members of the Clean
Plate Club all of the past six
weeks: Bobby Covington, Barbara
Inge, Gene McTeer, William Dom-
inick, Robert Freedman, Patricia
Pearce, Bill Whitford, Suzanna
Bozarth, Epes Robinson, Frances
Adkins, Elizabeth Maupin, Frances
Hix, Jimmy Williams.


     3B2 won the dollar given for
the highest percentage of parents
present at the October P. T. A.
meeting. Only four mothers were
not there.
```

Watts High Lights, November 1946.

Behavior in the cafeteria was always a matter of great interest; and around 1938, Mrs. J. A. Robinson, Supervisor of Elementary Schools, reported proudly in the *Durham Morning Herald* that

there has been much improvement in the arrangement of the lunch periods in the elementary schools. All the teachers and children now have lunch together. Table manners are observed, children taking turns of saying the blessing before meals. Some teachers sit at the table in the cafeteria with the children, while the other children who brought lunches eat in a special room with a teacher. In other buildings the teachers have their lunches sent to them on trays, eating in the classrooms with members of their group who brought lunch. Each building has its own plan. . . . At a stated time the children [who] have finished eating are excused and go to the playground.

Helen Burnett Coppridge '40 remembers

standing on the front main inside staircase to purchase our 5-cent green tickets that would cover the cost of a good hot lunch. Then we marched down the steps to the basement to go through the cafeteria line and to choose a seat at a table where we ate lunch with our friends.

We would hurry to finish eating lunch so that we could go to the playground for the rest of the period. Several of us girls owned large jumpropes, making smaller groups at each rope so we were able to enjoy more chants and jumping before returning to classes inside the building.

By 1944, cafeteria prices were: Meats 10 cents, Salad 5 cents, Vegetable 5 cents, Soup 5 cents, Milk 5 cents, Roll 5 cents, Dessert 5 cents, Ice cream 5 cents.

At George Watts School and throughout the country, World War II brought about patriotism, excitement, and the desire to help out our boys "over there." On 3 February 1942, less than two months after war had been declared, it was announced that all schools would begin Daylight War Saving Time beginning the following week. Geography classes soon began to take on special significance as students traced war developments on the large, pull-down maps. Eventually, nearly every classroom had several children who had brothers or cousins serving in the Armed Forces, an excellent reason for the class to compose cheerful, news-filled letters that would be mailed in a packet to the young soldiers. Air Raid drills took place occasionally; and at the urging of W. M. Coppridge, M.D., Chief of Medical Service for Civilian Defense, schools were required to keep First Aid supplies, and teachers to take Red Cross First Aid courses, in case of an enemy attack that would result in injuries to a great many children.

Along with all the other city and county schools, George Watts School regularly conducted newspaper collections and metal drives: such efforts were rewarded by contributions of metal of every kind, including keys, tooth powder tins, pots and pans, tin cans, even prized lead soldiers. (Eli Evans '48 recalls that he proudly became a Junior Commando when his household metal contributions were supplemented by an old furnace from his father's United Department Store.) In addition to making metal contributions, students conscientiously pasted 10-cent defense stamps into booklets that when filled could be exchanged for a $25 savings bond. In a speech to the PTA in April, 1943, Principal C. C. Linneman announced that George Watts School had collected 143,567 tin cans and 1,563 old keys, and had purchased $3,304 worth of war stamps and bonds.

Thrift now became the official stance of the nation; and "make it last," "conserve," and "do without" became the watchwords for George Watts students—as well as for the general population—for four years. Pupils dutifully took home information on nutrition ("How to cook with dried milk," "How to stretch half a pound of hamburger to feed four persons," "How to bake a sugarless, butterless, eggless cake"), as well as hints on growing Victory Gardens, information on the infinite complexities of rationing, and briefings on behavior during air raids. As well as discontinuing publication of *Watts High Lights*, students carefully saved their Christmas wrapping paper from year to year; towards the end of the war—when previous papers had become too bedraggled to use—they were decorating their own. When the war ended in 1945, most students were amazed by the sudden abundance of such luxuries as sugar, butter, and bananas, not to mention the disappearance of ration books. The Age of the Consumer had begun.

SCHOOL LIFE

* * * * *

With no antibiotics and few preventive measures available, communicable diseases were a matter of great concern during the first fifty years of the school's history. Due to the massive, nationwide influenza epidemic in the fall of 1918, all city and county schools in Durham were closed for six weeks: lengthened school days and shortened vacations were required to make up the time. Once such childhood diseases as mumps, measles, and chicken pox appeared, they ran rampant; in February of 1939, *Watts High Lights* reported, "Half of the children in the first grade have measles! The grade hopes they will all be well soon." Rheumatic fever, scarlet fever, and whooping cough were not infrequent, and tuberculosis excited much anxiety: health programs frequently stressed TB control, and each year the local TB Association sponsored essay and poster contests, as well as selling Christmas seals. Poliomyelitis epidemics occurred every few years, terrorizing everyone; in 1935 the city schools remained closed until 30 September, while again in 1944, the opening date was postponed to 18 September, both postponements due to widespread incidence of polio. Even the "common cold" was worrisome; and on 14 June 1939 a letter from Wilburt C. Davison, M.D., Dean of the Duke Medical School, was read in the City Board of Education meeting, criticizing the encouragement of "perfect attendance" in schools, because children were too often going to school with colds and other communicable diseases, and infecting their classmates.

Cleanliness, posture, and behavior received constant emphasis. Morning Inspections were held for many years in nearly every classroom; *Watts High Lights* faithfully reported the results, as in February of 1932 when the 5A1 reporter listed the names of the seven children who had had clean hands, clean teeth, clean fingernails, and clean handkerchiefs all year long. Usually Morning Inspection was followed by an opening prayer. Posture was of special concern: in 1932 Miss Olive Brown judged students' posture during Physical Education classes as well as elsewhere in the school, and pupils who passed the test were awarded a red tag with Good Posture written on it in large letters. The following year John Angier was chosen Good Posture Monitor, because, explained the *High Lights* reporter, "he carries himself very well." A perhaps inevitable disparity between boys' and girls' behavior patterns was indicated by a somewhat regretful report in October, 1929 that

> Twenty out of twenty-five girls in 5B2 made "A" on conduct and effort for October. Stewart Alexander was the only boy making the same.

Good behavior was conscientiously recognized, as when Table Four in 3B1 (1933) received the most stars for self-control. The *High Lights* applauded, "Hurrah for Frances Airheart, Jean Dermott, George Reece, Lela Taylor, Billy Marshburn and Merle Carver!"

During the first half of the twentieth century, school children—in both private and public schools—were allowed considerable freedom in skipping grades when teachers felt that their abilities warranted such action. One pupil who had begun first grade at the tiny, private Twaddell School when she was five was quickly moved to the second grade when it was discovered that she could already read; after completing third grade, she transferred to George Watts where—a shy newcomer—she started the fourth grade at seven. (Her mother accompanied her to school every day for two weeks to ease the difficulty of her entrance into this new and sophisticated world of public school.) *Watts High Lights* reported "skips" within its school with pride: in October of 1929, the newspaper reported that fourth grade teacher Miss Annie Garrard had been "trying" Lucie Lea Cavedo in the fourth grade for about two weeks, and observed, "We are glad to report that she stood the test and is now a real fourth grader. We shall miss her in 3B2."

For over two decades, the most coveted award that a boy could receive at George Watts School was the Jimmy Cannon Cup. First awarded in 1935 to Holland Young Holton, the silver loving cup had been presented to the school by Dr. and Mrs. James H. Cannon III in memory of their son Jimmy, who had died on 7 May 1934 while he was a fifth grade student at George Watts. The Cannons asked that the cup be awarded at graduation each year to the sixth grade boy who was deemed to have made the best record for grades, conduct, and effort. The recipient's name was engraved on the cup, which became his to keep during the summer; when school resumed in the fall, the cup was returned to the school to remain on display until that year's graduation exercises. In 1940, plans were announced to present a parallel award—the Lily Nelson Jones Cup—to the outstanding sixth grade girl; but perhaps because of war metal shortages, the cup was not awarded until 1946, when Caroline Garrett became the first recipient. Both cups were awarded at least through 1958, but it is not known what happened to them, or when the presentations ceased.

If one room could be said to be the heart of George Watts School, it would be—as Carol Seeley Scott suggested—the auditorium. There parents and teachers met for PTA meetings through the years; there pupils gathered to watch Lewis Gregory and Ralph Strayhorn star in the fourth grade's original production of *Marco Polo in China*; there they applauded Betty Lloyd Amis, Paul Parks, and Jane Phillips's performances in *Spring Cometh*, an original operetta written by fifth-grade teacher Mrs. Rhoda Kelley Hale; there they admired Annette Tilson and Ella Ann Proctor as they performed in *The Cobbler and the Elves*. There students heard local ministers explain the significance of Christmas and Easter, saw Wallace the Magician pull a rabbit out of a hat, listened to choral music and the Walter Damrosch orchestral programs, gathered to sing "We Gather Together" and to bring their canned goods for the needy at Thanksgiving. And there at last, one warm day in June, they marched down the aisle in long pants and white organdy dresses, two by two according to height, to sing the Vacation Song and to receive George Watts's diplomas and benediction before they entered the wider world of Carr Junior High, and "adult" movie tickets, and adolescence.

* * * * *

Epilogue

In August of 1996 George Watts School welcomed a new principal, John Colclough. In the preceding spring, reported the school's PTA Newsletter for October, the school had finished its year with 408 students. At the time of the Open House in August, preparations were being made for 450 students—the number that the building was designed to accommodate. By the third week in September of 1996, enrollment had risen to 554, a large percentage in the younger grades. During the following school year, 1997-98, the student population totaled 557.

George Watts is now one of three elementary schools in the Durham Public School system that are Accelerated Schools: such schools are actively involved in redefining themselves in order to better serve their students. The George Watts Elementary School PTA Newsletter of January, 1998 comments that the Accelerated School concept

> means that everyone in the community has a voice in what happens at the school. Committees, called "cadres," meet to discuss important issues.

Currently, explains the Newsletter, five working cadres—composed of staff, parents, and students—concentrate on the areas of School Climate, Curriculum and Instruction, Family and Community, Resources and Funding, and Discipline. Committees meet weekly to investigate problems, propose solutions, and make decisions on all aspects of school life.

The school playground was renovated during 1996-97. The area was drained and graded, and new playground equipment was installed.

The annual Fall Festival was held in October of 1996. Each class planned its booth: one produced a "decorate your own cupcake" booth, another offered a chance to "go fish" for prizes. There were other attractions: music, a "tattoo booth," a haunted house, a "cakewalk," a holiday booth, a children's puppet show, and a silent auction. A resounding success as usual, the Festival again took place in 1997, and gives every indication of continuing and improving with each new school year.

John Colclough, Principal of George Watts School, 1996-. Courtesy John Satterfield.

As a sign of the times, a program called "Safe Alone" was given at the school in March of 1997, providing information to pupils on how to protect themselves from danger when they were at home alone. When the speaker asked how many of the students assembled would be home alone later that day, between a third and a half of those present raised their hands. However, students who need before and after school supervision can report as early as 6:30 in the morning, and stay until 6:00 in the evening.

The George Watts Elementary School Wellness Center opened during the 1997-98 school year. The Center is a comprehensive school-based health clinic—only the second elementary school Wellness Center in North Carolina—whose stated purpose is "to provide students with all of the services they need at school to help ensure their physical, mental, and emotional health so they will attend school ready to learn and succeed." To this end, the Center offers a range of services including "care for students when they are ill, health screening and physicals, sports physicals, personal counseling, nutritional counseling, and a variety of school and community education programs."

The "Friends of Watts Street School" continue to provide funding for special school projects and equipment, as does the PTA, the school's oldest friend of all. With the strong support of parents, teachers, students, and Friends on its side—as it looks back over a proud history–George Watts School gazes confidently toward a bright future.

Notes on the Neighborhood

The "Trinity Park Neighborhood," which extends roughly from Buchanan Boulevard to Duke Street, and from Club Boulevard to Main Street, actually comprises many neighborhoods within its boundaries. To a child, the "neighborhood" usually extended no more than a block in any direction beyond his or her own house—the outer limits of the space that he or she was allowed to explore alone—so that each person had a different experience, different friends during his growing up. The common thread binding together the larger community during most of its existence has of course been George Watts School, its teachers, principals, and activities. But a few institutions, persons, and locations in addition to the school were common knowledge in earlier years to many in the larger neighborhood.

One of those institutions was the Watts Street Grocery at 1202 Watts Street, owned and operated from 1949 until 1979 by Ira and Frances Welch. (Owners during the few years previous to the Welches' taking over the business included Claiborne Berry, Jack Ennis, and Louis A. Lubow.) At one time or another everyone in the area went at least once or twice a week to this excellent small grocery store that offered fresh produce and bread daily; meats were cut by Ira Welch, while his wife Frances handled the cash register. The store was a particularly popular place for schoolchildren to stop by on their way home from George Watts School: favorite snacks included soft drinks, Popsicles, Hershey Bars, and penny candy (one enterprising young capitalist, Mike Troy, once bought out the store's entire stock of jawbreakers for one cent each, and sold them for two cents). In *Welcome Back To The Neighborhood*, a booklet compiled by Bill and Ann Kirkland for the 31 July 1993 neighborhood reunion, a number of former residents fondly recalled the grocery, and Ira Welch commented,

> We'd get most of our fruits and vegetables at the Farmers' Market in Raleigh. I'd get up at 4:30 in the morning and be back for breakfast around seven. We'd open the store at eight.

Buddy Whitfield recalled that his first job consisted of shelling butterbeans at Watts Street Grocery, while Raymond Weeks remembered enjoying a Moon Pie and an R.C. Cola on the grocery porch.

At one time or another, most of the children in the neighborhood made their way cautiously along the top of the stone wall that surrounded East Campus, puzzling over why no goldenhaired princesses were ever glimpsed outside the King's Daughters Home, and winding up their excursion by climbing the giant magnolia trees at the south end of the campus, close to Main Street. Usually they also checked the hand of the Sower statue for the pennies that Duke students occasionally left there, perhaps to ensure a good grade on an exam or to bring about a happy evening on a Saturday night date. Sometimes, after the children had climbed the magnolias to their heart's content, their mothers took them to the Dope Shop on the campus for a thick, cold, delicious milkshake; and then one more stroll along the stone wall before turning to go home.

The long hill on Markham Avenue between Buchanan Boulevard and Watts Street—with its huge oak tree in the center of the street—was always a popular place for sports. Betty Faucette Wilson remembers that

> the Recreation Department of Durham blocked [the street] off in the afternoons after school during warm months, and we neighborhood children used it as a free skating rink. How we could "crack the whip" around the lower side of that circle!

Likewise, she recalls,

> the Markham Avenue hill from Duke Street was blocked off during icy and snowy weather for sledding. The people who lived on the corner would run water down the hill in the evenings for very slick sledding. Adults and children alike joined in the fun with a big bonfire at the top of the hill.

Other former neighborhood residents remembered different, but also steeply-inclined areas where the daredevils in the crowd could perform on skates, bicycles or sleds: among these were the long hill on Buchanan Boulevard between Knox Street and Englewood Avenue, and the Knox Street incline between Watts and Gregson Streets.

Sooner or later, nearly everyone in Trinity Park went to the Duke Park swimming pool, a project of the Federal Emergency Relief Administration that had been formally transferred into Durham's possession in 1934. When you were little, your mother took you to the small, shallow, fenced-in "baby pool"; but when you turned six, you became an adult for Duke Park's purposes, and progressed to the "big pool" a few hundred feet away. After paying nine cents for admission in the chlorine-scented, wooden bathhouse, you received a wire basket in which to check your shorts, shirts, and sandals, and went inside a wooden booth to change into your bathing suit (and required cap, if you were a girl). A few athletic types actually swam and dove; but most young people went to Duke Park to see, to be seen, and to flirt.

Each August a crowd of several thousand enthusiastic onlookers gathered to watch the Duke Park water pageant, a fast-paced show that offered a brass band together with skilled divers and swimmers performing in straight and comic acts. Clowns lost their clothes in mid-air, or went into the pool in flames, while girls wearing seal costumes balanced balls on their noses as they executed a synchronized swimming act. Champion divers performed swan dives and double gainers that were rewarded by gasps of admiration, astonishment, and delight. One of the more popular acts was always that of the clown who rode a bicycle into the water in a dramatic but ineffective attempt to save a drowning man; the business-like three-year-old who eventually pulled the man to safety received one of the loudest ovations of the show.

Helen Burnett Coppridge, who grew up on Urban Avenue directly across from George Watts School, remembers that the girls in her neighborhood played jacks, Giant Step, and Red Light, as well as jumping rope; they swung, and slid down the sliding board (with the aid of waxed paper "to make the going faster") on the George Watts School playground. On warm summer evenings, parents sat on their front porches while their children played Hide 'n' Seek. Mrs. Coppridge recalls a particularly unusual neighborhood diversion:

> Families raised chickens in the back yard chicken coop. Each of us kids had a pet chicken that we named. At the end of the summer we had a chicken wedding including bride, groom, bridesmaids, and groomsmen, which we dressed accordingly.

The wedding organizers were so serious about doing it all correctly, she adds, that they sent invitations to their parents for the wedding.

Dr. John Glasson, who grew up at the corner of Markham Avenue and Buchanan Boulevard, across from East Campus, remembers that

> we had a neighborhood dramatic club, the Amateur Actors' Association. I was in it, along with Nancy LaPrade, Frances Briggs, Mildred Patterson, Louise Elizabeth Norris, and Pride Brown. Our parents acted as sponsors, and we presented plays in our homes. In the Breedlove home on Watts Street (their father

Trinity Park neighborhood baseball team, ca. 1930. Photo and identifications courtesy John Glasson, M.D. Members of the team include, Left to Right, Front row: Unknown, Fred Moore, Ran Few, Unknown. Middle row: Skip Alexander, Leonard Le Sourde, Horace [later "Bones"] McKinney, Bill Roberson, John Glasson. Back row: Bill Franck, Troy McKinney, Ken Few, J. B. Brame, Gordon Turner.

was a librarian at Duke), there were wide stairs that made fine bleachers for the audience while the play was presented in the entrance hall.

The Fullers, the Cheeks, the Delamars, and the Stallingses all had houses across from the school. The Fullers' house had a roof of wooden shingles that was always catching fire from sparks that flew out of the chimney.

Dr. Glasson also recalls his neighborhood baseball team—most of its players George Watts students—who played, he says, "in [Duke University] President Few's front yard."

Welcome Back To The Neighborhood, the book produced by Bill and Ann Kirkland for the 1993 Trinity Park reunion, includes a number of reminiscences by former residents of the neighborhood. Bev Barge, Bill Whichard, and others recalled the rock quarry and the woods that had stood where Northgate Shopping Center is now located. Several persons remembered the polio epidemics, and having to stay close to home during those times: Duke Park Pool was closed, and most mothers would not allow children to go to the movies. Joanna Holloway Nicholson and Nancy Llewellyn Towe confessed that they had built a clubhouse in Nancy's back yard, using lumber stolen from Jerry Gibson's house while it was under construction. And Michael May Lanning recalled the day Epes Robinson announced that he was giving a garage sale, and proceeded to sell his sister's toys to Michael and her three sisters. The girls spent their entire allowance, related Michael, and

> came home with dolls, doll clothing and furniture—many wonderful items. Unfortunately, Epes did not have permission to sell his sister's toys and later that day his mother came to our house and retrieved them. Unfortunately, also, Epes had already spent all of our money and we were never reimbursed.

If Epes attended the neighborhood reunion, Michael concluded, she hoped he would bring his checkbook.

* * * * *

Appendix

SCHOOL SONGS
(Reprinted from *Welcome Back To The Neighborhood*)

CLASS SONG

Dear George Watts—We love you so dear—
We'll think about you all through the year—
Dear George Watts—We love you—
And to you we'll be true.

Now the time of parting is near—
Farewell to you whom we love so dear—
Dear George Watts—We love you—
And to you we'll be true.

VACATION SONG

Is there anything you want to know?
Just ask us, we can tell;
We've studied hard for nine long months,
And we know our lessons well.
But now we're looking for the days
When we can have some fun,
For J-U-N-E always spells "Vacation."

Chorus

Then it's Hip! Hip! Hurrah!
For the good vacation time;
With an old straw hat, no shoes at all,
And a fishing pole and line.
The brook is calling to us,
And the woods repeat the tune;
The very air, without a care,
Says June! June! June!

PRINCIPALS OF GEORGE WATTS SCHOOL

1916-19	Jane Williams (Mrs. Jane W. Cobb)
1919-20 ?	Mrs B. S. Skinner
1920 ?-24 ?	Leah Boddie
1924-40	Lily Nelson Jones
1940-43	Calvin C. Linnemann
1943-45	Edward L. Phillips
1945-62	Lorraine I. Pridgen
1962-64	Gary R. Harris
1965-67	Charles B. Whitley
1967-72	Margaret F. Munford
1972-79	Ruth B. Rogers
1979-83	Margaret F. Munford
1983-87	Karen Chandler
1987	Wenda Adams (Acting Principal)
1987-91	Michael Courtney
1991-94	Delia R. Robinson
1994-96	Gayle Rasberry
1996-	John Colclough

THE JIMMY CANNON CUP

The Jimmy Cannon Cup, a silver loving cup, was presented to George Watts School in 1934 by Dr. and Mrs. James H. Cannon III in memory of their son, who had died on 7 May 1934 while he was a fifth grade student at the school.

Dr. and Mrs. Cannon's letter of presentation read in part as follows:

> We would like for the cup to stand on the desk of the sixth grade room throughout the year, and at the end of each year to have engraved on it under his [Jimmy's] name the name of the boy in the sixth grade who, during his course in the school, has maintained, along with good grades, the best record, as decided by the principal, for conduct and effort.

Winners of the Jimmy Cannon Cup, during the years for which information is available, were:

1935	Holland Young Holton
1936	Claude B. Williams Jr.
	Ben V. Branscomb
1937	Walter Faw Cannon
1938	Ralph Peel Rogers Jr.
	Charles W. Brame
1939	George K. Grantham III
1940	Walter Page Harris
1941	Alexander L. Blackburn
1942	William B. Anderson
	Duncan Morse Nelson
1943	M. Arnold Briggs Jr.
	David Baker
1944	James H. Davis Jr.
1945	Bobby Wyatt Wilkie
1946	Walter Shepherd Barge
1947	Carl Lloyd Cooper
1948	Gordon H. Rosser Jr.
1949	Carmon Harris Huckabee
1950	Donald Dupree Haithcock
1951	David Dillon Holt
1952	Robert S. Rankin Jr.
1953	John Otto Meier
	John McCool Dominick
1954	Dan Erwin

	Richard Reitzel
1955	Unknown
1956	Jonathan Francis Baylin
	William Hart Phillips
1957	Ray Bradley Jones
	Theo Clyde Manschreck
1958	Allan Rogers
	David Cox
	John Christian

THE LILY NELSON JONES CUP

In 1940, when Miss Lily Nelson Jones retired from her position as Principal of George Watts School, the school's Parent-Teacher Association voted to sponsor a loving cup named for her, to be awarded each year to "the best all-round girl finishing at the George Watts School," as Claudia Powe Watkins, Chairman of the Lily Jones Cup Committee, announced in a letter to the *Durham Morning Herald*. The Lily Nelson Jones Cup would parallel the Jimmy Cannon Cup for boys, which had been awarded at each graduation beginning in 1935.

Although plans for the girls' award were announced at the time of Miss Lily's retirement, apparently war metal shortages intervened; and it was not until 1946 that the cup was awarded for the first time.

Winners of the Lily Nelson Jones Cup, during the years for which information is available, were as follows:

1946	Caroline Knight Garrett
1947	Mary Margaret Weeks
1948	Betsy Carroll Lyon
	Nancy Sanders
1949	Charlotte Egerton
1950	Patricia Pearce
	Gwendolyn Cooke
1951	Sara Anne Way
1952	Myra Marische Cohen
	Mary Margaret Carroll
1953	Katherine Lee Pickrell
	Sandra Jean Norwood
1954	Rosalind Cooke
	Patricia Fisher
1955	Unknown
1956	Unknown
1957	Unknown
1958	Corrina Head
	Kathleen Hall
	Judy Atkins

It is not known when or why presentation of the Cannon and the Jones Cups was discontinued.

TEACHERS AT GEORGE WATTS SCHOOL

1917-18:

        Miss Jane Williams, Principal
        Miss Pattie J. Groves
        Miss Nellie McClees
        Miss Lillian White
        Miss Lela C. Newman
        Miss Ola Mae Ferebee

1919-20:

        Mrs. B. S. Skinner, Principal
        Miss Fessie Broadway
        Miss Marie Covington
        Miss Elizabeth Gray
        Miss Lucille Pearce
        Miss Virginia Puckett
        Miss Minnie Wilkerson

1929-30:

        Miss Lily Nelson Jones, Principal
        Miss Blanche Broadway
        Miss Helen M. Brown
        Miss Olive Brown
        Miss Blanche Burke
        Miss Ida Cowan
        Miss Olive Faucette
        Miss Annie Garrard
        Miss Ola Giles
        Miss Elizabeth Gray
        Mrs. Lorraine I. Pridgen
        Miss Verdie Trollinger
        Miss Marie Tyler
        Miss Elizabeth Walker
        Miss Lucy Royster, Health Nurse

1940-41:

        C. C. Linneman, Principal
        Grace J. Bishop
        Miss Blanche Broadway
        Miss Helen M. Brown
        Dorothy F. Coley
        Miss Ida Cowan

Miss Olive C. Faucette
Miss Elizabeth Gray
Miss Rhoda A. Kelley
Mrs. Lorraine I. Pridgen
Frances Rogers
Myrtle F. Tillman
Miss Elizabeth L. Walker

1950-51:

Mrs. Lorraine I. Pridgen, Principal
Miss Helen M. Brown
Miss Elizabeth Gray
Mrs. Mary W. Harward
Mrs. Helen B. Jones
Mrs. Eunice Mattox
Mrs. Agnes J. Moore
Mrs. Virginia H. Sanders
Mrs. Lois Sweaney
Mrs. Virginia H. Maultsby
Mrs. Marjorie N. Hughey
Mrs. Estelle W. Ridenhour
Anne V. Sutton

1960-61:

Mrs. Lorraine I. Pridgen, Principal
Mrs. Hilda D. Bell
Mrs. Elizabeth H. Bright
Mrs. Anne M. Brown
Mrs. Lou Ann Farrell
Mrs. Mary W. Harward
Mrs. Ava B. Hobgood
Mrs. Eunice H. Mattox
Mrs. Eva M. McArthur
Mrs. Agnes J. Moore
Mrs. Mary D. Nesbitt
Mrs. Virginia H. Sanders

1970-71:

Mrs. Margaret F. Munford, Principal
Mrs. Hilda D. Bell
Mrs. Virginia B. Bodiford
Mrs. Elia Clements
Mrs. Lyn L. Edwards
Mrs. Frances G. Few

Joseph Franklin Gibbs
Mrs. Mary W. Harward
Mrs. Ray Ann Johnson
Mrs. Mary D. Nesbitt
Mrs. Carole Q. Rice
Mrs. Nellie C. Settle
Mrs. Regina L. Tyor

EDITORS-IN-CHIEF, *WATTS HIGH LIGHTS*

1929-30	Mary Eleanor Krummel
1930-31	Jessie Ormond
1931-32	Elizabeth Gregory
1932-33	Frances Wade
1933-34	Elizabeth Dilts
1934-35	Mariella Hooker
1935-36	Ann Hamilton Roberts
1936-37	Walter Faw Cannon
1937-38	Caroline Lockhart
1938-39	Annette Tilson
1939-40	Barbara Barnes

Due to the wartime paper shortage, publication of *Watts High Lights* was discontinued during the 1942-43 school year. Publication resumed in October, 1946, a year after Mrs. Lorraine Pridgen had become Principal.

Since the available issues of the later newspapers do not have mastheads, a list of later editors-in-chief could not be compiled.

PRESIDENTS OF THE PARENT-TEACHER ASSOCIATION, GEORGE WATTS SCHOOL

(Known presidents of the organization are listed in chronological order. Where the year of the person's service is known for certain, it is indicated.)

	Mrs. W. H. Glasson
	Mrs. H. C. Satterfield
	Mrs. J. M. Ormond
	Mrs. H. D. Bitting
	Mrs. J. M. Cheek
	Mrs. H. W. Kueffner
	Mrs. James Cannon III
	Mrs. J. C. Angier
	Mrs. Frank B. Dilts
	Mrs. Marshall Spears
	Mrs. Milton Airheart
1938-39	Mrs. Thomas D. Wright
1939-40	Mrs. Wiley Forbus
1941-42	Mrs. George Hargitt
	Mrs. Deryl Hart
	Mrs. Robert N. Creadick
	Mrs. Gurney R. Blanchard
	Mrs. R. H. Potts
	Mrs. J. E. Maynard
	Mrs. James Davis
1946-47	Mrs. W. H. Llewellyn
1948-49	Mrs. Robert Creadick
	Mrs. W. Brewster Snow
1957-58	Mrs. James E. Davis
1958-59	Mrs. Robert D. Holleman
1966-68	Mr. Harry Rodenhizer (first male president)
1973-74	Mrs. Sarah Parrish (first black president)
	Dr. Curtis Eshelman
1995-96	Jim Campbell and Veronica Pettiford
1996-97	Jim Campbell and Kathy Sikes
1997-98	Alice Buchanan, Linda K. Harris and Kathy Sikes

SUPERINTENDENTS
DURHAM CITY SCHOOLS

It should be noted that Durham City and County school systems remained separate entities until 1992, when the two were combined to become the Durham Public Schools. George Watts School was a part of the City system for the first seventy-six years of its existence.

Durham City Schools Superintendents were as follows:

1885-1895	E. W. Kennedy
1895-1897	C. W. Toms
1897-1899	W. W. Flowers
1899-1906	J. A. Matheson
1906-1911	W. D. Carmichael
1911-1914	Ernest J. Green
1914-1923	Edwin C. Pusey
1923-1933	Frank M. Martin
1933-1947	W. F. Warren
1947-1958	L. Stacy Weaver
1958-1975	Lew W. Hannen
1975-1979	Benjamin T. Brooks
1979	Frank B. Weaver (Interim Sup't)
1979-1988	Cleveland Hammonds
1988-1989	Frank B. Weaver (Interim Sup't)
1989-1991	Hawthorne Faison
1991-1992	Joyce P. Edwards

Notes

For the most part, sources have been indicated in the text. Other references follow:

Chapter One. The Building in its Community

> Information on Durham and its commercial establishments in 1916 has been compiled from the Durham *City Directory* and the Durham *Morning Herald.*
>
> "Alice Burke and Nell Richardson. . . ." Virginia Scharff, *Taking the Wheel* (New York: The Free Press, 1991), 86-87.

Chapter Two. Principals and Teachers

> "[the students] went on to the wider world . . . ." Frances Gray Patton, "The *Terrible* Miss Dove," in *Twenty-Eight Stories* (New York: Dodd, Mead, 1969), 117.

Chapter Three. School Life

> Eli N. Evans relates his experience as Herod's tax collector in *The Provincials* (New York: Atheneum, 1973), 131.

Bibliography

Bueno, Belmira, Dempsey, Van, Hessling, Peter A., Noblit, George, Toppin, Reeda, and Courtney, Michael. *Coming Together: The Story of George Watts and Walltown Schools*. Durham, NC: 1989.

Edwards, N. A. *N.C. Congress of Parents and Teachers, 1919-44*. Volume I.

Evans, Eli N. *The Provincials: A Personal History of Jews in the South*. New York: Atheneum, 1973.

Holloway, Betsy. *Heaven For Beginners*. Orlando: Persimmon Press, 1986.

Holloway, Betsy. *Unfinished Heaven*. Orlando: Persimmon Press, 1994.

(No author listed, but compiled by William and Ann Kirkland): *Welcome Back To The Neighborhood: A Souvenir of Our Reunion*. Durham, NC: 1993.

Minutes of the Durham City Board of Education, 1915-1992.

Principal's Annual Report, Standard Elementary Schools, 1933-70. (Submitted to State Department of Public Instruction, Raleigh, NC).

Pulling, Steven T. *The George W. Watts Elementary School Renovation and Addition: A Case Study by Steven T. Pulling*. An unpublished study for an Architectural Conservation course at The School of Design, North Carolina State University. April, 1996.

Scharff, Virginia. *Taking the Wheel: Women and the Coming of the Motor Age*. New York: The Free Press, 1991.

Self-Study Report, George Watts School, April 1974.

INTERVIEWS

Margaret McCracken Allen
Helen Burnett Coppridge
Eli Evans
Cavett Hamilton French
John Glasson, M.D.
Mary Esther Williams Harward
Susan Harward
Dorothy Newsom Rankin
Robert S. Rankin Jr.
Rhodney Reade
John Satterfield
Nancy Llewellyn Towe
Warren Williams

WRITTEN COMMUNICATIONS

Helen Burnett Coppridge
Dorothy Newsom Rankin
Carol Seeley Scott

NEWSPAPERS AND OTHER SOURCES

Durham Morning Herald
The Herald-Sun
The Morning Herald
Watts High Lights

Scrapbook kept by Miss Lily Nelson Jones, n.d., but covering several years in the 1930s. (Courtesy of Louise Adkins and John Satterfield)

Index

(Illustrations in *Italics*)

INDEX

1994 Addition to George Watts School. Courtesy John Satterfield.

Original Watts Street School, 1916. Renovated 1994. Courtesy John Satterfield.

READ BIBLE VERSES RIGHT, PLEASE

One morning during morning exercises the sixth grade was having sentence prayers. Betsy Lawrence said, "Come right in after Virginia. Be quick, Lord, and we thank you for your son who was sent to save us."

The "come right in after Virginia. Be quick!" was part of the directions!

CHRISTMAS

A happy time is here again,
It's Christmas and a wish for all.
That He whose birth was on this
 day
Did reach the hearts of great
 and small.

May each of us help do our best
To make Christ's day a happy one.
And when we carry gifts to friends
They'll catch the spirit that
 our hearts bring.

For those whose souls have been
 downcast
Renew your hopes, look toward
 the sun.
For better times must be right
 here,
This Christmas time.

Bobby Gantt   6B2

STAFF PRESENTS HIGHLIGHTS QUIZ

Sarah Gaddy won first place in the first"Highlights Quiz" which was held in the auditorium on Monday, October 9. Meriwether Wright and Nancy Norton,members of the advertising staff, were in charge. Other contestants were Snowden Lyon, Paul Carswell, Charles Bridgers, and Sue Berry. John Taylor asked the questions and the audience supplied the answers which the contestants did not know.

Between rounds, Harold Andrews played "Il Trovoture" and Forrest Stinespring asked some tongue-twisters. Jean Roberts, business manager of HIGHLIGHTS, reported progress in the sale of the paper.

Anyone buying a copy of the paper is eligible for the quiz.

Watts High Lights, October 1939.

```
┌─────────────────────────────────────────────────┐
│                                                 │
│              Marked Down                        │
│                                                 │
│  Mrs. Nachamson: "Why is it,                    │
│     Billy, that you get lower                   │
│     grades in January and Febru-                │
│     ary than in December?"                      │
│  Billy Nachamson: "Because every-               │
│     thing is marked down after                  │
│     Christmas."                                 │
│                                                 │
└─────────────────────────────────────────────────┘
```

Watts High Lights, January 1935.

```
┌─────────────────────────────────────────────────────────────────┐
│                                                                 │
│                    5A2 SMOTHERS 5A1 21-5                        │
│                                                                 │
│       In a drawn out battle 5A2, with the help of many errors, walked │
│  over 5A1 21 to 5.  From the first it was a one-sided battle with │
│  5A2 pushing across the plate 5 runs in the first inning.  J. T. │
│  Boone did a fine job of pitching for 5A2, allowing only 6 hits, 5 │
│  runs, and striking out 5 batters.  He was backed up with fine field-│
│  ing by the whole team.  The line-up of the teams is as follows: │
│                                                                 │
└─────────────────────────────────────────────────────────────────┘
```

5A2 Line-Up

Position	Player	Hits	Times at Bat	Average
Catcher	Kenan Rand	0	4	.000
Pitcher	J. T. Boone, Captain	2	4	.500
1st Base	Marshall Spears	3	4	.750
2nd Base	Bobby Eblen	1	4	.250
Sh. Stop	Bobby Sugg	0	4	.000
3rd Base	Ralph Rogers	2	4	.500
Left Field	Thomas Huckabee	1	3	.333 1/3
C. Field	James Glover	0	3	.000
R. Field	Sam Moyle	0	3	.000

5A1 Line-Up

Position	Player	Hits	Times at Bat	Average
Catcher	L. H. Warren	3	4	.750
Pitcher	Charles McLamb	0	4	.000
1st Base	Chris Ferrell	1	3	.333 1/3
2d Base	Christy Delamar	0	3	.000
Sh. Stop	Billy Goodman	1	3	.333 1/3
3d Base	Jack Conway	0	3	.000
L. Field	Charles Slawson	0	3	.000
R. Field	Bill Houston	0	3	.000
C. Field	Hubert Howard	1	3	.333 1/3

Watts High Lights, May 1937.

Go Back Again

Marion was just home after her first day at school. "Well, darling," asked her mother, "what did they teach you?"

"Not much," replied Marion, "I've got to go again."

PEGGY'S SURPRISE

Peggy's surprise was a surprise for all of us in 6B2. November 14 was Peggy's birthday, and just when school was out Mrs. Hazel, Peggy's mother, came into our room with many packages. She told us not to leave, and we were glad to stay for we were anxious to know what was about to happen. Miss Brown told us to move our desks around the wall, and by the time we had done this Mrs. Hazel had put a lovely birthday cake on a desk in the middle of the room. We knew then what the secret was, and we could hardly wait for the ice cream we knew was coming. Mrs. Hazel gave us ice cream, cake, and the loveliest little baskets filled with candy. The cake had eleven candles on it and was so pretty it seemed a shame to cut it, but we are glad she did. We gave fifteen rahs for Mrs. Hazel, Miss Brown, Miss Trollinger, Mrs. Ramsay, Bobby Lee Hazel, Dorothy Hazel, Jimmy Hazel, Ruth Ramsay, and Miss Lily. The pupils of 6B3 enjoyed Peggy's party.

SOUVENIR

Sarah Speed was entertaining a girl friend of hers. They went in her father's study and there stood a skeleton.

"Where did your daddy get it?" asked the girl friend.

"Oh, he has had it a long time," replied Sarah. "I guess maybe it was his first patient.

Watts High Lights, September 1934.

QUIZZ PROGRAM

5B1 gave a program in the auditorium which proved to be very different and interesting.

The program was a quizz program on "How Well Do You Know Your School?" It was surprising how many children did not know the name of the P. T. A. president or the name of the Safety Patrol Captain. Betsy Lyon made an excellent mistress of ceremonies. Her assistants who picked out the contestants were: Margaret Hannah, Kay Penny, Frances Page, Margot Regen, Ina Russell and Jean Gerard. The program was made quite realistic by a real microphone on the stage. This was the courtesy of Mr. Maupin of radio station W. T. I. K. Mary Grace Maupin, Nancy Sanders and Nancy Llewellyn helped.

Watts High Lights, November 1946.

```
6B2 BOYS WIN VOLLEY BALL
        CHAMPIONSHIP

        The boys of 6B2 have again
won the volley ball champion-
ship.  The game was played with
5B1 on January 6th.  It seemed
easy for the sixth grade boys in
the first game, but in the last
two games the fifth grade warmed
up and gave them a battle they
will never forget.  The line-up
for 6B2 and 5B1 is as follows:


    6B2 Boys          5B1 Boys

Marshall Spears   Bradley Hender-
                            son
J. T. Boone       Eric Tilley
Bobby Sugg        Donald Fetna
Jack Conway       J. B. Cordon
Ralph Rogers      Harry Watkins
Charles Brame     James Codell
Kenan Rand        Buck Barber
John Huckabee     John Edwards
    Substitutes:
Francis Morgan
Charles Norton
Leon Dworsky
```

Watts High Lights, January 1938.

The Late Grandpa

```
Old Gentleman: (in office to
  Miss Lily) "May I please speak
  to Billy Smith just a minute?
  I am his grandfather."
Miss Lily: "You are too late.
  He has just gone to your fun-
  eral."
```

Watts High Lights, November 1934.